To d   ...ry

The Talisman
of Skerne
by Tom Carr

with love

Tom

ISBN: 146090222X
ISBN-13: 9781460902226

Dedication:

To Toni

Acknowledgements

To Toni, my wife, for her encouragement, many excellent suggestions, and for laughing in all the right places. To James and Lucy, my children, for the same. To Richard, my son-in-law, also for his appreciation and two notable contributions, too; and to Dave Carr, Bud Craig, Geoff Donaldson, Andrew Gladwin, Stephen Hughes, Angela Milligan, Hugh Mulrooney, Pete Shields, and Steve Wright for some shafts of wit I have "borrowed." Also, to Mike Jarvie, for two excellent contributions. He also kindly took upon himself the role of my first editor. His help was greatly valued. I would like to thank the team at Createspace—Gaines Hill, Margaret McCall, Caitlin McCann and Adam Miller—for helping me realise a dream. I reserve particular thanks for Ron Donaghe, for his expert, meticulous and sensitive editing. It was greatly appreciated.

Author's Foreword

An author I read in my youth was Dennis Wheatley—a writer of tales of Black Magic and derring-do. They were good fun.

However, they did contain elements of intellectual and social snobbery and, at times, quite blatant racism. I was never sure, either—I still am not—how seriously Wheatley took the supernatural subject matter of his books.

His tales, particularly "The Devil Rides Out," are the basis of much of the parody.

I hope by this foreword to avoid the fate of the creator of Alf Garnett, the mean-spirited, misogynist, bigotted central character in the 1960s BBC sit-com "Till Death Us Do Part." Some viewers of that well-observed satire saw the dreadful Alf as their spokesman.

I *may* have readers who habitually refer to Jews as "Yids," or who, for instance, *do* or did consider Mohammed Ali a "craven black" (Chapter Nine) because of his conscientious objection to the Vietnam War. Let me be clear that "craven" is the last epithet *I* would seriously apply to a man who faced Liston, Frazier, Foreman, *and* the might of the American establishment; and I detest racism of any sort. If there are such readers, I am *not* their spokesman! Let me repeat; the book is a *parody*.

I satirize other things in the book. Some Roman Catholics, maybe, will not like parts of it. But then they have the choice to take it, leave it...or even burn it!

However, I offer the book as a bit of light-hearted fun, as something that will entertain rather than offend. I hope it is enjoyed as such.

Tom Carr.

To my dear reader:

I have decided it may be kind—and certainly in no way patronising or pedantic—to supply a glossary of terms and references, in case you have missed one or two.

Chronology

Preface

It was an ordinary year, it was an extraordinary year; the usual things happened, unique things happened; it snowed in June in Britain, there was drought in August; summer was one of the longest and hottest on record, the start of winter was one of the coldest on record; Harold Wilson and Jacques Chirac resigned office, James Callaghan and Raymond Barre assumed office; Gerald Ford beat Ronald Reagan for his party's presidential nomination, Jimmy Carter beat Gerald Ford in his country's presidential election; Leonid Brezhnev was still Soviet leader, Mao Tse-Tung ceased to be Chinese leader; there were earthquakes on Earth, there was a space probe on Mars; train passengers travelled at high-speed intercity, plane passengers travelled at supersonic-speed intercontinental; chimpanzees became an endangered species; Microsoft became a registered company; the first recorded outbreak of Ebola occurred; there was a Swine Flu pandemic; the USA vetoed a UN call for an independent Palestinian state; the UK's Chancellor of the Exchequer borrowed 5.3 billion dollars from the IMF to deal with a budget deficit; there were dirty wars in South America, territorial wars in Africa, and the Cold War in the West; there was famine in Africa and India; there were terrorist attacks in the Far East, in the Middle East, in Uganda, in Canada, in the UK, in the USA; The Sex Pistols rode high in the charts,

Brotherhood of Man won the Eurovision Song Contest; Bjorn Borg and Chris Evert were Wimbledon Singles champions; Liverpool were Football League Champions; Southhampton won the FA Cup Final; Mohammed Ali was World Heavyweight Champion; Mao Tse-Tung died; my first child was born; so a year unlike any other; at the same time a year very much like every other. It began on a Thursday and ended on a Friday. It was a leap year. It was 1976.

The events that this book relates took place in that same year. It is as strange an account as any you are likely to encounter, and yet perhaps the strangest aspect of all is the fact that it has not been told until now. The world has remained in ignorance for a third of a century of a moment of peril as great as any it has ever faced. We have had the fission bomb since 1945 with its kilotons of destructive potential; the fusion bomb since 1952 with its megatons of explosive force. We have evidence now of meteor impacts that have released energy of several orders of magnitude even greater than these; catastrophes that have wreaked global havoc and brought mass extinctions in their wake. Nor are we yet, and perhaps may never be, free of the threat of any of them. Yet, the menace of all of these pales into insignificance, compared to the cataclysm one man could have unleashed had not the knowledge, intelligence, ingenuity, skill, and heroism of a mere handful of people unravelled and thwarted the abominable malefactor's wiles in the nick of time!

One reason this story has remained untold for so long is testament also to the character of each of our benefactors. None of them has ever wished to seek fame or fortune from their actions.

However, finally, here is their story. For its veracity, I will simply call to the reader's attention the old adage: "Truth is stranger than fiction!" It comes no stranger than this!

Prologue

Duc Théodore de Cornsai-Tantobé emerged from the rear, near-side door of his pristine, regal, black Bentley, which had just swept onto the long, paved drive, glided past the stately rows of trees—European Alder, Himalayan Birch, Lebanese Cedar, Siberian Elm, Japanese Magnolia, Canadian Maple, English Oak, Scottish Pine, Welsh Rowan, Cyprian Cypress—and purred to a halt outside the august portals of the French Noble's summer residence.

The *Duc* drew himself up to his full, imposing height, flexed his broad, lithe shoulders, and stretched his sculpted neck to dispel a little of the stiffness caused by the *longueur* of his journey. Then he stood transfixed for several moments before the weathered, limestone façade of the impressive edifice before him. Years of cultural refinement, intellectual rigour, and martial training could not wholly suppress the passionate, Gallic sensibility that was at the heart of the man. A single tear welled in the corner of one of his dark, intelligent eyes and coursed over the finely chiselled ridge of his cheek and down the side of his noble, aquiline nose before it was brushed away with a swift, subtle sweep of the long index finger of his aristocratic, well-manicured right hand. It was a tear of both joy and sorrow. Joy that he was again to spend time in the building's antique, labyrinthine interior, relish again its magnificent grounds and stride out daily into the rugged splendour of the Yorkshire Dales! Sorrow that the wife he had once had and the child she was bearing him would never share these joys!

His chauffeur had emptied and closed the car's cavernous boot and now waited upon the *Duc's* pleasure. Immediately, one of the two grand, carved, oak doors before them swung open and the *Duc's* Scottish housekeeper spread out her hands in heartfelt welcome! Though Flora McFlintloch had lived in Yorkshire for nigh on thirty years, her speech was unchanged.

"Och! The sight of yee both is e'en better than a gude dram of malt! It's sae gude to have the Laird back in his Castle!"

It was of no consequence that "Laird" and "Castle" were not strictly correct. The noble *Duc's* heart surged with affection as strong as that a nephew could have for a favourite aunt at the sight of this plump, ruddy-faced, homely woman.

"And Flora, may I say, the sight of you is better than the rarest, vintage *armagnac*," rejoined the *Duc* in his distinctive, deep, resonant baritone with that *soupçon* of *Sacha Distel* that might even have charmed the pants off her (had he so wished)! He advanced and placed three kisses on her cheeks, and his chauffeur did likewise.

"Och, get away with yee both!" She always made a show of submitting reluctantly to this "slobbering" as she called it, but always her cries of protest could be heard mere millimetres away! For *she* held for *both* of these men affection as strong as that an aunt could have for a favourite nephew.

"It's so good to be back here, Flora!" continued the *Duc.*

"Och, that's gude tae hear! Now in you come. You'll know where to put those, *Jean*," she added to the chauffeur, indicating the suitcases, "and then a cup of tea, or a wee dram, or whatever you will."

"Tea for me, please, Flora," responded the *Duc.*

"Oh, a 'wee dram' for me, please," replied the chauffeur. "It's been a long voyage."

"*Jean*, I've told you before, 'journey' would be better!"

"*Eh bien!* 'Journey.' The 'wee dram' would be better still!"

"And how are the pets?" asked the *Duc.*

"Och, they're fine. Young Angus"—she referred to her grandson who lived locally—"sees to them for me, and he's muckle ta'en wi'em, they're sae ferlie! He looks in on them everyday. They're well cared for, dinnae fash yersel', Sir!"

"Splendid," said the *Duc*, whose mastery of the Anglo-Saxon languages extended even to their most outrageous dialects! "I'll just look in on them too while you're making the tea. *Jean*, you'll dispose of the suitcases?"

"*C'est déjà fait.*"

And so the three of them went for three different reasons to three different parts of the building, but all three were seated together around the kitchen table three minutes later, each on one of three chairs, to enjoy one of two drinks.

"Flora," the noble *Duc* announced after his first cup of tea, " the two of us would like to freshen up first, but I'm sure we could eat a little something very soon afterwards. What have you in store for us?"

Flora told him.

The previous evening, this seasoned man of the world had dined in one of Paris' finest restaurants on Atlantic Marbled Grouper poached in a *court bouillon* with a coriander leaf, fennel bulb, caper, and *Chablis* base, which he had washed down with vintage *Hautré-Wattisse champagne*. This had been followed by honey and ginger *sorbet*, a speciality of the house.

And yet, now, he was savouring with no less anticipation the prospect of one of Flora's staple, seasonal dishes: ham hock with pease pudding, neaps and tatties, and a side salad of diced, raw swede and radishes, sliced beetroot, and grated carrot, topped with Heinz salad cream, which he would wash down with some Mullard's "Auld Arthur" stout. This would be followed by summer pudding, one of Flora's favourites[11]…but such was this wholly exceptional man's latitudinarian disposition!

"As always, you spoil us," he said with utter sincerity.

"Och, get away with yee," said Flora a second time, and like the first time, with sincerity somewhat less than utter!

"Flora," continued the *Duc*, "we shall have guests in about two weeks time—yes, the American and the Russian! So we must consult and plan, and have done anything that needs doing before then, so perhaps we can sit down together for an hour or two tomorrow to discuss

---

1   And of all who ate it!

all this? *Oui?* Tonight, though, I simply want to unwind and just enjoy being here. *Jean,* I suspect, may venture into the village later to renew an old 'acquaintance.'" And at this, the *Duc* and Flora exchanged a knowing look, as knowing as such a look can be.

"Of course," said Flora. "The meal can be on the table within half an hour!"

Half an hour later they dined splendidly.

The *Duc* and Flora made plans over coffee at ten o'clock the following morning.

"Sir," she said, eventually, "aboot the curtains in the east drawing-room. Och, the colour's well faded; they probably do need replacing."

"Of course, Flora. Just ring the suppliers—they should still have the measurements. If not, they can come and re-measure. Then order identical replacements."

There was a poignant pause, as poignant as such pauses can be.

"Taupe?" Flora finally said, and in such a way that the monosyllable slapped the *Duc's* cheek like a glove. "Och, Sir, is it no time for a change?" She had made her challenge. "I've got their latest catalogue, and they've got some real bonny, new colours!"

Several seconds elapsed before the good *Duc* replied.

"I take on board what you're saying…I know where you're coming from…"—the French Aristocrat's grasp of English was truly astounding—"…and I totally understand why you want to flag up this concern, Flora, and run it past me. But, please understand, I'm just not ready to go there yet..." At which, a distant look came into the *Duc's* dark, intelligent eyes.

It could *not* be said that the garden of the *Duc's* life was at present *without* variety, colour, or abundance; yet its central trellis—where once was entwined the most exotic of blooms—was still bare. Gone was that garden's most resplendent and focal glory. The bright, elusive butterfly of love could no longer be in thrall to its alluring iridescence or gorge on its intoxicating nectar; and the *Duc* felt himself thus irredeemably bereft!

Taupe had been his wife's favourite colour, and it remained here and in his *château* in France, too, a symbol of her abiding presence in his heart! He was still not prepared to relinquish this.

"I'll talk to you about it again, soon, Flora, I promise" said the *Duc*. And Flora knew when to beat a strategic retreat. One could lose a battle yet still win the war!

But little did the good *Duc* know that, even as he spoke, not much more than a hundred kilometres to the northeast of his present location, strange events were about to unfurl with which he would unexpectedly become embroiled and which would change his life forever!

PART ONE

Chapter One

In a little-known, eastern backwater of County Durham, between the coastal village of Crimdon Grange and the mining village of Trimdon Colliery, lies a tiny settlement forgotten by time and cartographers called Grimdon Lea, referred to locally as "Grim." Hidden in a deep hollow, surrounded by trees and farmland, it consists of a terrace of cottages and a medieval, Roman Catholic church: that of St. Polycarp, the patron saint of garden ponds. Yet despite a regular attendance at Sunday Mass of only six people, the parish boasts a permanent priest *and* a sexton, each maintained there by the Vatican itself. Why this should be so is a mystery to every other cash-strapped, overworked parish priest across the whole of the diocese, though—it must be said—to scarcely anybody else, apart from one other, whom we shall meet in due course!

As our story starts, a young man called Stanley Crook has not long been appointed to the recently vacated post of sexton, and is just settling into the unfurnished cottage that comes with the job. On the anticipation of his first salary, he has just splashed out on his newly acquired Barclaycard and bought some of Habitat's *"Matty The Builder"* range of starter furniture. He has prioritised the kitchen/diner. In it now are four *Herby* stools. These are in the shape of tall, empty, upended crates; and to put on the *Herby* stools, there are two

Alby cushions covered in strong, cotton fabric printed with the motif of a Portland Cement bag, and two *Kev* cushions covered in the same fabric printed with the motif of a Gypsum Finishing Plaster bag. *Dave*, the table, is a simulated, overturned building brick palette supported by two trestles. Screwed to a wall is *Mick*, the coat-hook rack—four six inch nails protruding from a rectangle of two by four soft wood. Next month, Stanley hopes to get two capacious *Ernie* beanbags for the lounge. Each is roughly the size, and bears the motif, of a "Magnet Southerns" soft sand dumpy bag. To stack and display his collection of books, he intends to buy *Bert*, which bears an uncanny resemblance to one hundred building bricks supporting four scaffolding planks. With all of these furnishings he dreams of impressing Cheryl, the barmaid at his new local, if ever he manages to lure her back to the cottage to see them. So far, he has only managed to stutter his order to her, then sit with his glass of beer in a corner of the bar casting furtive, longing glances over the top of a newspaper at the splendour of her cleavage as she pulls a pint.

But in all other respects Stanley could not believe his luck. Not only had he managed to stammer complete answers to all the questions in the interview, he had actually been offered the job over the heads of older, more experienced and vocal applicants.

And the job itself was so good; indeed, the pay was exceptional, given what the job entailed! The church's tiny graveyard was full, so there would be no grave digging. Cleaning the church, arranging six prayer books, six hymn-books, placing six weekly parish bulletins on the table at the back of the church before Sunday Mass, tending the grounds and carrying out the very few other routine, weekly maintenance tasks was neither difficult nor time consuming. So he found himself with lots of freedom to indulge his personal hobby: devising board games.

His first—"Evolution"—had taken him a year and a half to complete. Waddingtons had complimented him on the originality of the concept, the subtlety of the rules, and the high quality of his graphics. The aim of his game was to be first to arrive on the square "Homo Sapiens." But if, for example, a player found him or herself on the evolutionary pathway to becoming a newt, he or she needed to throw a six to reverse direction. In the end, though, his submission had been turned down. Waddingtons' principal objection was that "Evolution" just took so long!

But nonetheless they had encouraged him to continue with his ideas. His latest project was called "Calvary." He thought it propitious that he should have landed a job with the Church when embarking on such a scheme. The aim of *this* game was to be first to arrive on the square "Resurrection." Currently, he was close to completing the graphics for the square: "The Veil of the Temple is rent in twain—miss a turn."

Little did Stanley know that his stammer, his solitary nature, and his time- consuming hobby were strong factors in his favour. He was considered the "lowest risk" candidate in the whole field by the appointing body.

Only after his appointment had he learned the crucial role he would be expected to fulfil, and thus the reason for such seemingly disproportionate investment in the parish and the job. He was to be co-guardian of artefacts deemed so dangerous by the Church that their whereabouts had to remain secret at all costs. To this end, he had had to swear a solemn oath on the Bible in the presence of a Vicar-General *and* sign a legal document in the presence of a judge! By learning this secret, he left only the cash-strapped, overworked parish priests across the whole of the rest of the diocese—plus the one other—still puzzled by the parish's exalted patronage...unless the unsuccessful candidates for the job were wondering about it just a bit as well.

It was Friday. At four o'clock, as required in his contract, Stanley went dutifully to the doors of the church. The parish priest, Fr. Donal O'Hegarty, was already there.

"And are you getting well settled in, Stanley?" the cleric enquired.

"Y...Y...Yes thank you, F...F...Father."

"You sound a bit stuffed up, Stanley, have you a summer cold?"

"N...N...No, Father. H...H...Hay f...f...fever."

"Oh, now is there anything worse?"

Stanley felt he did not know his immediate superior well enough yet to suggest that Cholera or Bubonic Plague were, if anything, worse. He smiled instead.

"Are you ready?" continued the priest.

Stanley nodded. It saved time. The church doors were already unlocked and the two entered. They went to a door at the rear of the nave which bore in red letters the legend: "NO ACCESS TO THE PUBLIC." This, too, was already unlocked and open and the stairwell lit. Together, they descended a stone, spiral staircase into the crypt. Once at the bottom, both could now see facing them a metal safe bolted to the far wall.

The safe was a recent addition and greatly simplified the precautions the two men had to take. In decades, indeed in centuries past, other procedures and means had been employed. Well aware of Man's fallen nature, and the reason for his fall, the Church took practical, as well as moral and legal, means to ensure its edict regarding the contents of these artefacts remained inviolate. On learning their infamous nature, Pope Bonilace[2] I in 1153 had issued a decree that no other should ever cast his or her eyes upon them. But! Forbidden fruit! What killed the cat! Therefore, religious and legal oaths were sworn, the former incurring infernal, the latter, swingeing financial punishment should they be broken. But, additionally, means were also devised whereby no *one* person could have access to the artefacts, and a rich reward promised to the tempted should he reveal if ever the other became the tempter. For centuries, the combination of such ploys had been successful.

Stanley advanced towards the safe. Fr. O'Hegarty remained where he was. Stanley selected each number of the six-digit code for the safe, which only he knew. It was also written on a sheet of paper in an envelope in a bank vault, which would only be retrieved and opened upon his death or his quitting the job[3], so that the code

---

2   The name and the pronunciation are French.

3   In fact Stanley was unaware that all the recent sextons had died before retirement age. It must be said that this included one young man who had stated his intention of resigning but who soon

could be reset to the new sexton's secret specification. Stanley then stepped back and Fr. O'Hegarty stepped forward and inserted a key into the safe's keyhole. Fr.. O'Hegarty opened the safe, then turned aside and beckoned Stanley to look at what they were surely still guarding. Stanley could see the quite ordinary, old, wooden chest.

"Is it there?" asked the priest.

"Y...y...y...yes, F...F...F...Father. It is."

Now the priest looked inside the safe. This was the ritual. "Indeed, so it is," intoned the priest. "We can rest easy." There was a moment's pause. "Would you not like to know its name, Stanley? Do you not fancy having a little peek inside the chest?" he continued unexpectedly.

"N...N...N..." Stanley shook his head and slammed shut the safe. "It's f...f...f...forbidden that I sh...sh... sh...should."

"Well done. You pass the test," said another Irish voice, and a figure emerged from the shadows of the crypt's stairwell. Stanley had never seen this person before, had been totally unaware of his presence, but recognised at once the red robes of a Cardinal.

Fr.. O'Hegarty turned his key and locked the safe. "Your Eminence," he said, "I think you'll agree we have chosen well."

"So it would seem," said the other, as though Stanley was no longer there. "At the present moment, this is crucial. There is a recent resurgence of interest

---

afterwards slipped and plummeted to his death on Blackhall Rocks one Saturday evening——a tragedy about which deep sorrow was publicly expressed at Sunday Mass the following day by the Vicar-General who was visiting the parish at the time.

in this...this...obscenity. Its security is now doubly imperative!" He abruptly turned towards Stanley and signed him a blessing. "Well done, young man! You stood your ground! The role you have here is of extreme importance. I feel confident we have placed it in good hands. God bless you, my son. I am also sure you realise that Fr. O'Hegarty's offer was not a genuine temptation—merely a test—and therefore you have no claim on the reward"

"Of c...of c...of course not, Your E...Your E...

"God bless you again. You'll not mind at all then signing a disclaimer as soon as we're back in the presbytery."

"N...n..."

"May God bless you thrice." Whereupon the Cardinal began to mount the stairs.

Fr. O'Hegarty followed, the key held firmly in his right hand. Stanley had copies of all the keys for all the doors of the church...but not for that of the safe! Where Father O'Hegarty kept this key was a secret, as closely guarded by *him* as was the safe's code by Stanley. On this matter, Fr. O'Hegarty was subject to the same checks and inducements as his new sexton.

Later, seated comfortably atop a *Herby,* padded with a *Kev,* Stanley swigged a celebratory beer straight from the bottle. All in all, he was well pleased with what had just transpired. Also, plans were forming in his head for a modified dice for his game of "Calvary"—tiny crucifixes replacing the usual dots that denoted the numbers. He would begin work on this in the morning.

Chapter Two

Fr. Donal O'Hegarty's view of his own position was more equivocal. Offered the parish just after he had turned sixty, he realised the job would give him a great deal of time to himself to pursue his own interests. There would be no burials. Baptisms and weddings were highly unlikely. And he had only one sermon and one bulletin to write each week. Confessions, it turned out, though, were not overly interesting. Given both the small size and the advanced age of his congregation, time behind the purple curtain was largely without any sins of impurity to savour. In the case of the one exception, he would have preferred that it followed rather than proved the rule. What the dirty old buggers saw in each other was as confounding as what they still managed to get up to! And the images thus conjured up, the poor priest found disgusting rather than erotic. But no matter.

Over the previous three months, Fr. O'Hegarty had re-read all the novels of Dickens and was now re-embarking on a personal favourite Fielding novel: *Tom Jones*. It's not unusual that this should be so, since his post-graduate specialism had in fact been the Eighteenth Century English Novel.

Nor would it be too long before he would be digging up this year's potato crop and setting about distilling another vat of *poteen*. He was also relieved that the visit of Ireland's latest Cardinal had really been quite perfunctory, so he had neither had to feed His New Eminence nor guide him through a tour of the presbytery that might have revealed his still and his cellar.

A serious drawback to the post, however, was its rural location. Things of which he was mortally afraid surrounded Fr. O'Hegarty. This was a cross he had long had to bear and that had cost him dearly! In most of the adjacent fields there were cows. When with young calves they were dangerous beasts—and just behind the presbytery, in the field, across which there was a public footpath, the local farmer regularly and maliciously put a *Limousin* bull. It was a beast of enormous bulk and awful menace.

But also, occasionally, swans visited the nearby beck, and Fr. O'Hegarty knew for a fact that an enraged swan could break your arm with a beat of its wing.

At tupping time, Fr. O'Hegarty would even avoid fields with sheep in them. There might be an aggressive ram running with the flock, and these had been known to break legs with one butt of their heads.

Fr. O'Hegarty was terrified of dogs, of which country folk kept many. When they growled and bared their teeth at him, their owners offered a range of observations, none of which calmed Fr. O'Hegarty in the least: "They can scent fear, Father, that's why they growl at you"; "They're testing to find out your position in the pack, Father, you have to show them who's boss"; "He's just a playful puppy, Father"; "He has a sense of humour, Father."

Then there were cats. Their faeces could infect you with toxoplasmosis. Bats bothered him; the hideous creatures might even have crossed the channel carrying rabies—he wouldn't put it past them!

Whenever he found a relatively safe rural path along which to amble, Fr. O'Hegarty nonetheless always took his walking stick with the cloven end and wore Wellington boots, his precautions against adders.

He fretted about rats and catching Weil's[4] disease from their urine, which they may have left anywhere. He had once been told that wherever you were in England, you were never ten yards from a rat[5]!

Worst of all, though, were wasps, much worse than bees, which were bad enough, but bees had their uses. Not only did wasps sting horribly; they tested his faith! He had huge difficulty fitting them into a scheme of Creation designed by a Beneficent Creator. He constantly told himself that he, a mere mortal, should not presume even to grasp, let alone question, the entirety of God's Overarching Purpose. He would say decades of the rosary to distract himself from these thoughts. He had even once scourged himself with bramble stems to allay these doubts. But this niggling worm of a question would not stay wholly buried. Why did wasps exist? What was the point of wasps? What in Heaven's name had He been thinking about when He created wasps? (And bats!) Perversely, the query would inexorably resurface whenever the plagued priest encountered a wasp, or a *hornet*—that *baroque* wasp! The mere thought of *hornets* made him blench and tremble. Why, will be revealed!

But, there was a wasp buzzing around the picnic table when Fr. O'Hegarty stepped into his garden the

---

4   Pronounced "vile"—which, as diseases go, it is.

5   The Reader must make of this statement what he or she will.

morning after his rendezvous in the crypt with his new sexton and Ireland's new Cardinal. He had somehow to get past the abhorrence to get to where he wanted to go. Little did he know, however, that the vespine interlude that was about to unfold would be observed from a nearby copse. Binoculars were even then trained on the presbytery garden, and what the watcher saw, the watcher found intriguing and felt may even have great potential!

Fr. O'Hegarty suddenly swayed back and waved his arms, like a boxer riding and parrying punches. Still like a boxer, he ducked suddenly into a crouch and then bobbed and weaved rapidly, before back-pedalling at great speed to and fro along the side of the table, still apparently dodging or swiping away the blows of an invisible foe seeking to trap him against equally invisible ropes.

The man with the binoculars at that point could only hazard a guess as to who or what the invisible foe might be, but the utterances of the priest were carried to him through the clear, morning air.

"Abomination! Go away! Go *away!*"

Suddenly, the priest turned tail and bolted back into the house. The watcher waited. Presently, the priest reappeared carrying a fly swat. The watcher was again rapt. So, obviously, some sort of flying insect! The priest was clearly on the offensive now. "Where are y', y' nasty little bugger? Ah, *there* you are! Die! *Die!*" He thrashed the fly swat violently onto the table, and then leapt back abruptly. "Feck! You bastard! Just settle! Settle! *Die!*" The fly swat crashed again onto the table. "*Yes!* That's put paid to *you*, you little twat!"

Having removed one small part of His Maker's creation from this world with immense satisfaction, Fr. O'Hegarty returned the fly swat to the house, then as quickly re-emerged and made his way round the side of his dwelling towards the church.

Cautiously, the watcher stepped out from the copse into the field and began to approach the presbytery. As he did so, the *Limousin* bull and the herd of cows with their young calves, which were quite close by, took stock of him. Suddenly aware of them, the man stopped, turned, and stared at the bull intently. For a few seconds, the bull returned his stare, then slowly turned its head, lowed softly to the rest of the herd, and began to lead it away from the man to the farthest extremity of the field.

The man continued his walk up to the presbytery's garden gate. He opened it and inspected the picnic table. On it was a flattened wasp. "Ah, so that was what *that* was all about! Mm. Much as I thought!" Rather amused by what he had just perused, he mused, "This might be something I could use!" Already in his mind was the germ of a diabolical ruse. He was enthused.

He re-entered the field so that any passer-by would see him join the road via the stile from the public footpath.

He had come to this place as the result of an astute suspicion. How ever occasionally puzzled the rest of the parish priests of the diocese might be, nonetheless they were probably so cash-strapped and burdened with other cares that they had neither the time nor the energy even to think about, much less try to resolve, the enigma. But with the man it was otherwise! He suspected that here was a ploy of such Machiavellian subtlety only a medieval, Papist mind could have conceived it. The very obscurity, anonymity, downright nondescription of the place could be the very reason it had been considered the choice location to hide the things that in fact he sought. He did not yet know for sure that they were here, but he strongly suspected they were, and he was already pondering ways in which he could verify it was so!

But also this cunning and malign person already knew the true nature of the things he sought. He had been one of a very small number of individuals over the centuries that had ever managed, covertly, to penetrate closely guarded archives and scrutinise proscribed documents and thus discover what had caused that Pope so long ago to wish to keep these things forever secret. And, consequently, now he lusted after them as a wolverine lusts after fresh flesh, as a vampire bat lusts after red blood, as a dugong lusts after ripe cranberries.

He walked slowly up the narrow country road, crested with tufts of grass—so infrequently was it used—past the presbytery towards the church. The priest was standing just inside the church grounds engrossed in conversation with a young man. As the man passed unnoticed, he heard the poor young man's stutter, but also the priest ask the young man how he was enjoying the role of "Sexton," and ask, too, the young man's opinion of "The Golden Cock"—the inn at the crossroads a mile or so from Grimdon. The man pretended to tie a shoelace to give himself time, unseen, to hear the young man's reply to this smalltalk. The young man finally finished saying that he liked the job and enjoyed going to the pub on a Sunday evening when it was quiet. This, the man duly noted.

The man's orange *Citroën GS* was parked half a mile farther along the road. Already, the man's mind was teeming with schemes. It was still only mid-morning. He would go to Middlesbrough. He would look for some bee-keepers' equipment, a child's fishing net, two lidded jars—one large, one small—and a means of printing those things that were only just springing to mind. The first few items were easy to find. His last requirement took a little longer to source, but much of the time he spent searching for it he also spent rehearsing and refining the tale that it would support. Eventually, he found what he wanted. He was very pleased indeed with what the day had produced.

Neither Fr. O'Hegarty nor Stanley Crook had the slightest idea that their conversation had been overheard and had become the basis of nefarious plans as they went about the rest of their day. Stanley worked on his board game. Fr. O'Hegarty read some more Fielding and supped *poteen*.

The man, meanwhile, had returned to a cottage nearby that he was renting and unpacked his purchases. He drained a large jar of pickled gherkins of their vinegar, jettisoned the vegetables into his waste bin, steeped the empty jar in hot water and washing-up liquid, and prised holes in its lid with a screwdriver. This had been the biggest jar he could find. Then he had scooped out fish paste from another jar and jettisoned its contents, too, into his waste bin and left this empty jar to steep in hot water and washing-up liquid too. This had been the smallest jar he could find. He had kept the lid, but done little to it other than clean it.

He was thus prepared for an activity he decided would best be left for later the next week. He was more eager to see what tomorrow evening would bring. He continued to rehearse the tale he then hoped to tell.

Chapter Three

During the course of Sunday afternoon, Stanley had had another idea for his game of "Calvary" with which he was well pleased. There would be a square called "The Two Thieves." Next to it would be a rectangle on which would be placed ten cards, face down. Five of the cards would bear the words: "Good Thief"; five of them would bear the words: "Bad Thief." The cards would be shuffled before the start of each game. The player who landed on the square "The Two Thieves" would have to turn over the top card from this pack. If the player turned over a "Good Thief" card, then he or she would go immediately to the square "Resurrection" and most likely win the game. If the player, on the other hand, turned over a "Bad Thief" card from the top of the pack then he or she would go back to the square: "Jesus is scourged at the pillar—miss two turns" and would have to do so before resuming the uphill struggle all over again.

The redesigning of the dice, the graphics for the various squares, and now these new cards were all coming along wonderfully. Stanley even wondered for a fleeting moment around half-past six how many other geniuses throughout history had stuttered.

Stanley also had another source of personal pride— his teeth. They were white and perfectly formed. They were subject to a particularly vigorous brushing before he left for the pub at around twenty to seven.

A particularly sunny July had just merged into an equally splendid August across the whole of England and, so, Stanley's mile or so walk to "The Golden Cock" was idyllic. The trees were gloriously leafy and the hedgerows burgeoning with wild flowers, whose subtle perfumes Stanley's nostrils could still capture with rapture despite his allergy. Birds gaily trilled all around him; crickets merrily chirruped. And—consequently, maybe—a spring of courage welled in his breast that tonight he might more than just stutter his order of a pint of bitter, please, to Cheryl. There was so much more he would like to say to her.

Stuttering, though, he often thought, is like trying to be really cool with a sexy French chick when you've only got O-level French.

Stanley longed to invite Cheryl back to his cottage to show her his board games, but knew at the same time that such a chat-up line would be naff beyond belief, doomed to certain, ignominious failure, even if he could finally complete it before she lost the will to live!

But, on the other hand, there was the anguish that it was by no means certain any of his games would ever be accepted and marketed by any established firm. So, unless he formed his own production and distribution company—a daunting prospect he had never really seriously considered—then all of these things in which he took such pride would never be appreciated by anyone else, unless he himself showed them to someone else himself. And he would so much like that someone else to be Cheryl, rather than Fr. O'Hegarty! Stanley was on the slopes of the foothills of the mountain called "Desperation."

Cheryl was in the act of pulling a pint when Stanley came into the bar, and the sight of her splendidly-revealed cleavage gave him chills that were multiplying... he was losing control! He knew at once that curbing his stutter just then would be an Everest to climb. But he was relieved to notice that the table in the corner where he usually sat was free.

The man she was serving, who was seated on a bar stool, was someone Stanley had not seen in the pub before. He was a squat man, wearing a white, crumpled, three-piece, linen suit. Stanley noticed a gold watch chain disappearing into a pocket of its waistcoat. The man's head was totally bald; he had flat, lobe-less ears, bulging eyes almost amber in colour, and his chin merged into his neck with the merest ripple of a change of contour. His skin had a sallow, parchment-like quality, and the teeth he revealed as he smiled at Cheryl were crooked and yellow.

Cheryl placed the man's drink before him, took his payment, and returned his change. Then she turned her attention to Stanley. "Hello again," she said, giving him a knee-weakening, scrotum-tightening smile. "The usual?"

This was so nice, not just the recognition and the remembrance, but she had minimised what he would otherwise embarrassingly have had to attempt to say. Stanley was almost in love. He could have quite simply nodded, but was in fact determined to say, "Y...yes please." He had no idea why, but, hay fever or no, "yes" was much easier to say than "pint." Strange!

"You sound a bit stuffed up," she continued. "You can't have a cold in this weather, surely!"

"N...n...n...no, h...h...h...hay f...f...fever."

"Oh! There's nothing worse."

Stanley would have so loved to say to her, "Well, actually, Smallpox and Botulism are nothing if not very much worse," and smile at her knowingly, impressing her with both his wit and his teeth. Instead, he only displayed his teeth in what approached a smile. Stammering his thanks, he paid her, picked up his change, his drink, and the newspaper that was usually somewhere on the bar, and then went to the corner, just to ease his pain. He could have added that, compared with hay fever, stuttering, too, was very much worse.

He had not taken any more than three disconsolate sips from his pint and smoothed the front page of the newspaper, when he became aware that the man who had been on the stool at the bar was now standing next to him, pint in hand. Stanley looked up at him.

"Excuse me, but would you mind very much if I joined you for a few minutes, please?" asked the man and smiled his snaggled, yellow-toothed smile, which was the very antithesis of Stanley's own.

Stanley had detected a slight foreign accent, though the man's English seemed fluent. "N...n...n...not at all."

"Allow me to present my card," the man continued and handed Stanley a business card on which was written:

Jacques Frelon
Speech and Language Specialist

"I 'ope you don't mind, but I could not 'elp 'earing your stutter. This 'ole field is my speciality...I just 'appen to be in the area visiting a fellow academic at Durham University. I am currently embarked on a doctorate studying atypical phoneme delay in stutterers. If you would be prepared to 'elp me in my research, I might be able to be of some 'elp to you. I 'ave for some time also been developing techniques that are already showing encouraging results in alleviating your problem. In case you are interested, my masters thesis was on *typical* phoneme delay in stutterers—not a widely known paper, I freely admit, but reported in scientific journals, I assure you, as a seminal work of great importance. For, of course, one must first establish the norm before one can describe the abnormal. You can surely appreciate this, *non?*" For a fraction of a second, the man feared he might have just over-egged his cake, but no! Stanley was avid!

"Y...y...yes! B...b...b...but th...th...thanks. Wh...wh...what w...w...would it in...in...in...involve?"

Stanley had been impressed that the man had waited patiently for him to finish each utterance, not anticipating what he was trying to say and finishing it for him as so often happened, and which always fomented in Stanley's mind visions of acts of brutal violence. So, in addition to the straw—any straw—at which Stanley would grasp when offered, this also inclined Stanley to consider the man's proposal very favourably.

"I would want to spend some time with you, ideally in comfortable surroundings, with a tape recorder and record your speech. This would be both data collection for my study as well as diagnostic—to determine the best sort of intervention to offer you. I would also offer you some relaxation techniques. The first session would take, per'aps, up to an hour. After that, per'aps two, maybe three shorter sessions to instruct you in the techniques to practice and use. 'Ave you any time tomorrow?"

Stanley nodded vigorously.

"Excellent! Then maybe tomorrow afternoon, for example. Around two?"

Stanley again nodded vigorously.

"Where?"

"M...m...my pl...pl...place?"

"That would be ideal. And where is that?"

"J...j...just a m...minute." Stanley produced a pen from the inside pocket of his light, summer jacket and drew a map and wrote his name, address, and 'phone number on the back of a beer mat.

The man took and examined it for a moment then disconcerted Stanley with another snaggled, yellow-toothed smile. "Yes. That's quite clear. Thank you. Now I must go. Until two tomorrow then, Stanley." And he rose and offered Stanley a hand to shake. The spring of enthusiasm that was welling to overflowing as a result of this encounter drained somewhat through the sluice of disconcertion when the experience of shaking the man's hand resembled, for all the world, that of grasping a handful of maggots.

Stanley drank more beer.

Unusually—and maybe because of the conflicting feelings he had just experienced—Stanley decided he would have another pint. When he got to the bar, a slim, young man of medium height was already standing there. Cheryl was in the process of pulling *him* a pint. The splendour of her cleavage was already affecting Stanley deeply, and would again soon when *he* ordered *his* pint. Mm! Cheryl eventually turned her attention to Stanley with another knee-weakening, scrotum-tightening smile.

"Do you know that guy who was just talking to you?"

"N...n...n..."

"Didn't you think he was a bit creepy? He reminded me of a toad."

"He sounded to me more like a 'Frog'," said the slight, young man. He followed this with a braying laugh.

Cheryl gave him the briefest of glances, her expression neutral.

Stanley merely shrugged. "Another p...p...p..." he began.

"Pint," said the slim, young man.

Stanley clenched his fists and nodded.

Cheryl flashed the man a look that seemed wholly one of annoyance. With splendidly displayed cleavage, she began pulling a weak-kneed, scrotum-taut Stanley his second pint. Then she said to him, "You're becoming a bit of regular. Have you moved into the area, then?"

"Y...y...y...yes." He handed her some money.

"Whereabouts?"

"Gr...Gr...Gr..."

"Grimdon Lea," said the man.

Stanley ground his teeth. Cheryl flashed the man the same look and then turned to the till to get Stanley his change. Little did Stanley know, but Cheryl was greatly relieved that this man was leaving the following morning. If only there'd been no room at the inn when he'd arrived. He had been a pain in the arse each night he'd spent in the bar. In an accent that sounded to her like a quacking duck, he had repeatedly told her he was taking his first holiday in the North, as if by doing so the region was hugely in his debt! He was a garden gnome salesman from Twickenham! He drove a Ford Zephyr! He had a two-bedroomed flat above "The Rawalpindi"! He only had to pop downstairs to get an Indian meal! He narrated these facts, as if it were inconceivable, upon assimilating them, that she would not very soon beg him to whisk her away at once for a dirty weekend in Twickenham that included the nightly delights of exotic food. All in all she considered him an odious little turd.

While Cheryl was still occupied at the till, Stanley gulped a good two thirds of his pint, determined now to leave as soon as possible.

Cheryl gave him his change and asked him: "Do you have a job locally? What do you do?"

Stanley nodded. "Sex…sex…sex…"

"You manage to get some round here, then?" said the man, following this with another braying laugh and a suggestive look at Cheryl.

Cheryl's eyes rolled upward and, saying to Stanley, "Oh, excuse me, just a minute, please," she turned again and needlessly reopened the till to give herself time for her annoyance to subside.

"Sexton," Stanley finally said to her exquisitely shaped rear.

Stanley then downed the rest of his pint in three swift gulps and turned and kneed the young man in the groin. His victim whimpered, slumped forward, and clutched desperately with one hand at the bar top to save himself from falling. His other hand was already cradling his excruciatingly painful parts.

Cheryl turned, aware that something had happened. She saw the doubled-up, purpled-faced young man gasping for air, and she saw a dazzlingly dental smile on Stanley's decidedly handsome face. Then she saw his empty glass.

"My God, that was quick!"

"I was thirsty," said Stanley. "See you again soon."

Slowly, a smile and a slight pinkness that Stanley unfortunately missed spread across her face.

As he walked breezily but sneezily down the leafy, pollen-heavy lane back to his cottage, he decided he would ask *Jacques Frelon* tomorrow if he had any data on how the incidence of stuttering among prisoners banged up for Grievous Bodily Harm compared with the incidence in the general—generally non-violent—population.

Chapter Four

Who was the more eager to see the other, Stanley or the man who called himself *Jacques Frelon*, is moot. No matter, the two individuals greeted each other effusively at the front door of Stanley's cottage at the agreed time.

Stanley's guest entered the cottage and placed a briefcase and a small cassette recorder on *Dave*. Having looked at the rest of Stanley's new furniture, he was extravagantly complimentary "Oh! This is excellent! So imaginative! I cannot believe a designer in Paris would ever have the audacity to think of such a range...Very clever! We could learn so much from you English at this time..."

Stanley showed him the catalogue. "Mm! *Alby, Bert, Herby*...such names!" he exclaimed with such appreciation.

Stanley was charmed. "C...c...c...can I off...off... off...offer you a dr...dr...dr...drink?"

"What are you going to 'ave?"

"I pr...pr...pr...prefer b...b...b...beer."

"A beer would be very nice, thank you."

Stanley brought two glasses and a bottle opener to the table and then went to the fridge. He returned with two bottles, uncapped them, and poured them into the two glasses. As Stanley took the two empty bottles away, however, the man who called himself *Jacques Frelon* emptied a sachet of powder into the glass nearest Stanley. It needed time to dissolve, so the man immediately engaged Stanley on his return in plugging the cassette recorder into a socket, and then in having a tour of the rest of the cottage.

Eventually, the two returned to the table and took a sip from their beers. The man noticed Stanley raise his eyebrows momentarily after his first sip, then shrug and take two more hearty gulps.

"Right," said the man. "Are we ready?"

Stanley nodded, again to save time.

The man resumed. "I 'ave 'ere a passage of prose that I would like you to read and which I will record. But let me first explain. It is—or at least I 'ope you find it so—deliberately dull. This is because subjects that excite us, or indeed even inflame us, create for the stutterer an added dimension of difficulty...that of 'eightened emotion. I want to remove that added dimension and see what your...'ow shall I say...your base level is. You understand?"

Stanley nodded.

From his briefcase, the man took a laminated sheet of A4 and handed it to Stanley. He then put fingers on the PLAY and RECORD buttons of the cassette recorder and said to Stanley, "Nod when you're ready."

Stanley nodded.

The man pressed the buttons. And Stanley began to read aloud the following:

The wheel hubs of the *Citroën GS* are bolted to pivoted, trailing arms at the ends of each axle. Connected to each trailing arm is a cylinder containing a piston, above which is hydraulic fluid under pressure, delivered or removed by the opening and closing of inlet and outlet valves controlled by the movement of the front and rear anti-roll bars. Near the top of each cylinder is a damper valve, which regulates the rate at which the hydraulic fluid passes into or out of a metal sphere attached to the top of the cylinder. The sphere contains a flexible rubber diaphragm, against which the fluid pushes. Above the diaphragm in the upper part of the sphere is Nitrogen gas under pressure, which acts as a spring.

Only single-minded pursuance of his pernicious goal sustained the man's patience throughout Stanley's perseverance in completing this entire passage.

Stanley drank more beer when he had finally finished, which greatly pleased the man.

"Now," continued he who called himself *Jacques Frelon*, "I want to record—and of course analyse—your response to the anticipation of rhyme and rhythm, to see if in fact *you* personally find it 'elpful or not. You English 'ave these poems called 'Limericks', *non*? I 'ave some examples, but if you 'ave a favourite, that would be better."

Stanley nodded. "B...b...b...but it's v...very r...r...r...rude!"

"Most of them are. *N'importe!* But would you first write it down for me, please?"

Stanley did so, and it must be said, with some glee. This is what the man eventually read:

"There was a young Bishop from Birmingham,
Who liked to fuck girls when confirming 'em.
He'd pull up each nightie,
And praise The Almighty,
And pump his episcopal sperm in 'em."

"I see what you mean," said the man with an air of interested, yet professional, detachment. "Mm, the assonance in the final line is very clever!" Clearly, the objective judgement of a trained expert in language! Stanley was both gratified and impressed!

Inwardly, though, the man was exultant at such a ribald and irreverent insinuation of the Clergy's depravity. He was also consequently warming somewhat towards Stanley. An unaccustomed twinge of remorse was stealing into his heart at the cynical use he was making of this afflicted young man, and he made an unprecedented, charitable decision before he enclosed himself again within the carapace of his malice. His usual instinct was that the only Good Samaritan was a dead one.

He resumed his charade. Again, the cassette recorder was activated, and he waited patiently throughout Stanley's performance. Again to the man's gratification, Stanley drank more beer when he had finished.

"I now want to see what 'appens when that anticipation of rhyme exists, but is frustrated. Again, I will use the medium of the 'Limerick,' except this time, it is in some respects a 'Non-Limerick'. 'Ere, you will see what I mean. Please read this."

"There was a young man from Tralee,
Who was stung on the neck by a wasp.
When asked: "Did it hurt?"
He said: "No, not at all,
It can do it again if it likes."

Stanley began a third, protracted recording. When this was finished, the man was fulsome in his praise of Stanley's efforts. They finished their beers. All the while the man was watching Stanley closely and had not long to wait before the hoped-for signs appeared: a languor in Stanley's manner, the dilation of his pupils, his smile of inner contentment.

"That is my data-collection finished. I cannot thank you enough. Now, can I move onto the relaxation techniques of which I spoke? I would like, of course with your permission, to attempt some hypnosis. I cannot guarantee it will completely eliminate the stutter overnight, but it will certainly eliminate any anxiety the stutter generates and this, of course, will be hugely beneficial. Are you willing to consent to this?"

Stanley felt so at one with the world, he did not hesitate for a second. The man removed his gold watch from his waistcoat pocket and began to swing it slowly before Stanley's eyes. The man's voice became a soporific susurration, and within less than a minute, Stanley was in deep hypnosis.

Less than three minutes later, the man who called himself but was *not Jacques Frelon* knew all that Stanley could tell him—the secret, six-digit code, the Friday afternoon ritual, the whereabouts of the keys to the church, the contents of the safe and the other key, which was in the safekeeping of the priest. The man was also now wholly convinced that he had found the things that he sought and that would very soon be in his grasp. Then, after he had erased all recollection of what had passed from Stanley's mind, that tiny, unexpected diamond of kindness within the granite of his heart led him to put his present power over Stanley to altruistic use.

A little later, when instructed, Stanley emerged from his trance.

"How do you feel?"

"I feel great. Totally relaxed. Thank you," Stanley said, without the slightest hesitation. "Oh my God! Wow! *Thank* you!"

"Please, please! Not yet. Let me caution you. You are presently unusually relaxed because of what 'as just 'appened. There will probably be some regression, as that wears off, and especially in difficult or stressful situations. We still 'ave some way to go, more work to do. Can I suggest the same time next week for another session, and by then, of course, I should 'ave an in-depth analysis of your recordings, which will point to other techniques we could employ. *Eh bien*, I take my leave. Until next week."

As the man sat in his car and replayed the recording he had made of Stanley's revelations, he smirked horribly and emitted a mephitic, croaking chuckle.

Stanley, meanwhile, was playing music, prancing round and round *Dave* and, between sups from a second bottle of beer, declaiming to the walls of his kitchen/ diner a fluent stream of the things he would very soon say to Cheryl.

Chapter Five

Donal O'Hegarty's ordination had inaugurated a ministry on which the Irish Catholic hierarchy had pinned great hopes. The scion of a wealthy and respected Dublin family, Donal had been a student priest of outstanding promise and had gone on to obtain a First at Trinity in Theology and then a Masters in English Literature. His sermons proclaimed that he was one clearly "blessed with the blarney." He was also arrestingly handsome, with that striking, Celtic combination of raven locks and piercingly blue eyes! What was more, he was endowed with a particularly fine tenor voice. Some had even started to dub him "The Caruso of the Cloth!" A solo rendition of Bach's "Ave Maria" that Donal was called upon to deliver one Good Friday in Dublin Cathedral was of such aching beauty, grown men had wept openly and nuns had fainted in their pews. Here was someone clearly destined to go far…

Yet, grotesquely, it was a sole visit in his youth to the farm of relatives in Connemara wherein lay the serpent that eventually would banish him from his promised Eden. And, indeed, a real serpent was its source! An adder bite had dispatched his aged, great-aunt Dympna, which was why his parents had taken him there.

It was the first time Donal had left Dublin. It was the first time Donal had seen a dead body. He filed past the open coffin behind his great-uncle Fergal—Dympna's youngest brother—and heard him murmur, in admiration of the embalmers' skill, "Oh, to be sure, if she'd looked as well as that when she died, she'd be here celebrating with us now!"

It was later during the wake, as Guinness and *poteen* loosened tongues, that Donal learned Fergal himself had narrowly escaped death only days before by vaulting over a dry stone wall to avoid a charging bull. Such athleticism at such an age merited toasting. More Guinness and *poteen* flowed.

"Did no one ever tell you," his Aunt Bernadette asked him not long after this, "that the countryside's an awfully dangerous place? Did you know that cows can be worse than bulls when they're with young calves? And let me tell you, as well, when I was nine, my arm was broken by a wild swan at Coole!" And she did tell him, in excessive and gruesome detail.

She it was who had also warned him when he first arrived to keep clear of "Paisley," the Irish Wolfhound on daily sentinel duty, tethered by a long leash to a fence post near the farm entrance. "Now, take my word for it, he's not what you'd call a sweet-natured pooch, Donal. Not at all! He once ripped out the throats of two Alsatians!"

In the barn were feral cats that hissed and spat when anyone entered. Aunt Bernadette had advised him never to try and stroke them. Young Seamus—a half-cousin—had done so and had been ill for weeks with "Cat Scratch Fever."

Alone in the tiny box room—where he slept on a straw mattress beneath a crocheted quilt—on his second night there he had looked out of the window at dusk and seen a bat, something he'd never seen before. It was hanging in the eaves, stretching its wings prior to taking flight. He had been horror-stricken! It was like some grotesque creature you might find lurking in the corner of a painting by *Hieronymous Bosch*. For the first time, but not for the last, a vague unease troubled the mind of the devout young Catholic about aspects of the Almighty's Grand Design.

And then on his last day there, a wasp had stung him! It was as if a hot needle had been thrust into his arm, but the searing heat took an age to abate. The sole consolation offered to him (by Aunt Bernadette) had been, "Ah well, it could have been worse...it could have been a hornet!"

He had returned to Dublin, and not long afterwards, entered the Seminary. Memories of these rustic horrors quickly faded as he began to excel in his chosen path. He was embarked, it appeared, on an almost assured rise to ecclesiastical greatness.

Almost, but not quite! The young curate was close to mastering "Nessun Dorma" in the bathroom of the presbytery of his first parish in Dublin, when a 'phone call from none other than Ireland's own Cardinal brought him hurrying downstairs in his bathrobe.

"Yes, Your Eminence?"

"Ah, Donal, hello. I hope I've not caught you at an inopportune moment! No? Oh fine! And how are you?

Good. Good. Now I don't know how clear I've made this so far, but let me do so right now. I recognise you as a young man of exceptional talents, and I'll not shilly-shally about by pretending that I haven't got great plans for you! Yes indeed! I'll not go into too much detail at this point, and I'll trust you to remain discrete on the matter. I have your assurance on this, Donal, don't I? Yes. Good. But listen. The rise I foresee—your rise—must not be seen to be too...meteoric...do you follow me? Certain folk—I'll not say who—must not be given ammunition to wag fingers, either at you or me. Do I make myself clear? So, I'm afraid you must be seen to have had some experience wider than that of the Seminary, Academe, and Dublin—a more 'catholic' apprenticeship, if you like; please pardon the pun. I've decided to appoint you as a curate to a little country parish in County Sligo. You'll only be there for a few months and then back to Dublin and onwards and upwards. I'm sure you'll see the logic of this, Donal; I think it's for the best."

"Of course, Your Eminence!"

In truth, Donal could not really have said otherwise. Nonetheless, he was too flattered by so overt a declaration of the Cardinal's favour and was also beginning to congratulate himself smugly that here, too, was an opportunity for a very public and exemplary display of humility, that he had not even begun to think for a moment what County Sligo would be like.

But Connemara was what it turned out to be like! Quickly, his anxieties about the dire natural dangers all around him that Aunt Bernadette, the bat and the wasp had implanted, but which had long lain dormant deep in his psyche, re-emerged with a vengeance. After only three weeks, as he went about visiting the elderly and the sick in remote cottages that were guarded by dogs or infested with cats, past grazing beasts with young on his way to and from farm houses, returning home late in the bat-laden dusk, passing the beehives in the local convent where he said a weekly Mass, it was all he could do to keep in check his stomach-churning, knee-weakening terror!

And then catastrophe struck on the Tuesday afternoon of Donal's fourth week in the parish.

At this point, however, I would like to tell the Reader something of that local convent, to which was attached a small, girls' convent school. The nuns were Sisters of Mercy[6] presided over by Mother Inviolata, a formidable woman with facial warts and hair and an elephantine bosom. In those days, Irish nuns held their priests in great esteem. So their almost conditioned response to the new curate had been to make a big fuss of him. But Mother Inviolata's demeanour soon began to change. The regular presence of this young man, with the beauty of a Greek god and the voice of an angel, was starting to have a clearly disruptive

---

6   The Author once heard it said——though he can no longer remember by whom—that this was possibly the worst misnomer in History, and had the Order been founded in the time of Merlin and Morgan Le Fay, it would have been named: "The Nuns Perilous." A scurrilous libel, without doubt, but perhaps of some interest to the reader.

effect on her whole institution. The schoolgirls would become quite "bold"[7] on the days he came to say Mass, but even some of her own order, young nuns previously so meek and obedient, started to become skittish and giddy when he was around. At the core of her being, Mother Inviolata passionately held an imperishable tenet of faith: "Here abideth Faith, Hope and Chastity; but the greatest of these is Chastity." She had very soon concluded that Donal was a cause of impious, prurient thoughts; he was a grievous occasion of sin! "By their fruits ye shall know them!" Then disaster struck Donal, and at once, Mother Inviolata saw in this quite clearly the hand of God!

The Tuesday afternoon in question had been particularly sultry. Donal had walked far afield in the course of his duties and was sweaty from exertion and fear (he had had several close encounters with potentially highly dangerous animals). He decided round about three-thirty in the afternoon that he would soak in a warm bath before changing into fresh clothes. When the bath was ready, he decided it would be a good idea to have also some fresh air waft through the bathroom, which he knew was not overlooked. However, the ancient casement had not been used for some time, and it took Donal some pulling and pushing before it suddenly swung wide open and out of his grasp. As it clattered against the outside wall, it unfortunately dislodged a hornets' nest. At first Donal was only aware of an angry buzzing, then one,

---

7   One of the most damning indictments a nun can utter!

42

then three, then many more of the irate insects appeared outside the open window. The memory of that burning wasp sting and the ominous words of Aunt Bernadette returned: "It could have been worse…it could have been a hornet." Now, here was a myriad, about to come into the very room where he stood with every square inch of his flesh exposed to their vicious venom! In a state of extreme dread, deprived of any ability to think rationally, all Donal could do was respond to the flight instinct. Without a thought of grabbing his bathrobe, he leapt out of the bathroom onto the landing and bounded down the stairs as the enraged swarm invaded the house.

The Author will again digress for a moment, with the good Reader's indulgence.

As we have seen, Nature had been prodigal in the gifts She had showered on this young man, but there was one area in which She had been capriciously negligent; Donal's donker was decidedly dinky.

It was on the frenetic flapping of his podgy, little todger that Mother Inviolata's horrified gaze finally fell, as the stark-naked Donal bolted in blind panic down the presbytery's front garden path towards *her*, Sisters Carmel and Fatima, and their cohort of school girls out on a ramble to collect wild flowers for the convent chapel's altar.

43

The Talisman of Skerne   by Tom Carr

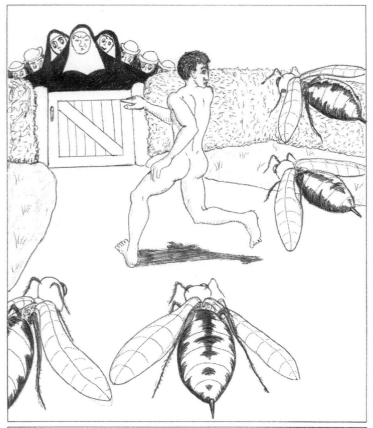

It was on the frenetic flapping of his podgy, little todger that Mother Inviolata's horrified gaze finally fell...

44

Fr. O'Donnel, the parish priest, an unworldly and kindly man, was occupied for some time caring for his new, young curate, whom he had found in a pitiable and still-naked state, huddled in a corner of the presbytery garden. He had then had to find someone who could deal with the swarm of hornets infesting his house.

Mother Inviolata, however, had lost no time in putting the worst construction possible on what had occurred to the Cardinal himself, who it just so happened was a younger cousin she had unrelentingly intimidated as a child. "It's absolutely beyond question! He cannot remain as curate here a moment longer!" she had concluded.

Donal was summoned forthwith back to Dublin.

It would be an overstatement to say that Donal had made enemies there, but he quickly discovered that he had few friends. Even as he emerged, clearly crestfallen, from his meeting with His Eminence, the Cardinal's secretary said with seeming innocence, "A fall from grace, Donal? So that's the size of it, then!"

Word had got around.

Indeed it had! It has been said that a joke coined in Glasgow on a Saturday night is going round the pubs of London the following Tuesday and is being told in the bars of Sydney within less then a fortnight.

✥

Who made public Donal's penile impoverishment and the history of its discovery remains unknown. Mother Inviolata herself? Sisters Carmel or Fatima? Or one of the bolder convent-school girls?[8] No matter. Within much less than a fortnight, however, it was known throughout the Emerald Isle!

He had become a laughing stock.

✥

He was summoned again by the Cardinal two weeks later.

"I'm sorry, Donal. What's happened has happened. It's been said even the Almighty cannot change the past! The best thing for you is to get away from here completely, have a totally new start, somewhere where you have no history. I've arranged a curate's post for you in Quebec. Now, what do you say to that?"

"What can I say, Your Eminence?" At that point Donal would have appreciated the offer of any escape. But the sudden prospect of rebuilding his status and career across the Atlantic in a modern, vibrant city inflamed his imagination immediately. "Of course! Your Eminence, I cannot thank you enough!"

"Bless you, Donal, and God speed."

The Quebec to which the Cardinal was sending him, however, was Quebec, County Durham, a tiny, ribbon

---

8   If we assume—as seems reasonable—it had to be one of them, this however raises the question: how had she a means of comparison?

settlement on a windswept ridge ten miles or so from the city of Durham itself. Dogs, cats, bats, adders and stinging insects abounded, alongside human inhabitants Donal could barely understand; and everywhere around his new home were fields full of cattle, sheep, and bizarrely—just to further compound his problems—on one particular farm, alpacas. One specimen of this species of South American camel—which resembles a sheep designed by a committee on LSD—had spat at Donal over a wall as Donal walked by. Within a month, Donal had had a comprehensive nervous breakdown and was confined for a long period to a hospital run by Sisters of Charity[9].

Ever so gradually, however, Donal was able to resume his priestly duties—though only in urban settings—again as a curate, then as a parish priest, and finally as Catholic chaplain to one of Durham's colleges, where books and people of learning surrounded him again. This, particularly, had helped his passage through anger, bitterness, and frustration, to a resigned acceptance and ultimately an inner peace. So much so, that he, who had once dreamt of being Eire's own Papal Emissary, of hearing the world's finest tenors at the Teatro dell' Opera and La Scala and who knows, perhaps, of even becoming one of their number, was able to reflect that the joy he had given to an audience of forty-three when

9   Deemed by the same scurrilous source already referred to, as possibly the second worst misnomer in history.

he had played Frederick in *The Pirates Of Penzance* for the Ferryhill Operatic Society was no less worthy...

On finally being offered the sinecure of St. Polycarp's, he had known what steps he must take to reap its benefits. The presbytery windows would never be opened. Aerosols of insecticide would be positioned strategically in every room. A fly swat would be within arm's reach of his bedside; another always on the kitchen table. The one farm he must visit, he would do so by car, and drive to within a foot of its front door. He would tell *all* his parishioners he was allergic to cat and dog fur, and would they duly oblige him by banishing all pets from his presence when he visited, please? Except in extreme emergencies, he would not go out after dusk, when bats were emerging from their roost.

It could be said then to be, very nearly, a happy ending.

Chapter Six

Very nearly, but not quite.

For Donal and Stanley, the next Friday dawned with great promise. The splendid summer weather continued unabated.

Donal appreciated it through the closed windows of his study, as he typed his weekly bulletin onto a Banda master from which he would roll six copies well before noon, the appointed hour for his first glass of *poteen*, just before a spot of lunch, and then some more *poteen*, as he relaxed for the best part of the afternoon with his Fielding.

Stanley appreciated it as he deadheaded the flowers in the churchyard, bagged the odd scraps of litter, fallen twigs or leaves, and watered the parched grass. Sneezing was a small price to pay, for the warmth and dazzling light were glorious.

Later that afternoon, their brief, weekly duty would be quickly and uneventfully dispatched.

What was more for Stanley, his stutter had barely returned. Tonight, he would go to The Golden Cock and *talk* to Cheryl; seriously chat her up; wow her with his wit, teeth, and talent; he, a cool *boulevardier* now to her sexy French chick. O-level French? *Pas du tout!* Seriously fluent *chic, Ma Chérie! Mais oui!* Metaphorically speaking, of course.

oⲰo

Less than three miles away, the man who called himself *Jacques Frelon* was placing bowls of strawberry jam on the garden table of the cottage he was renting and savouring the promise of the day with similar relish. An hour later, wearing gloves and a beekeeper's netted hat, he returned to his bowls of jam, with his fishing net and his two jars. He used the net and the smaller jar for entrapment, the bigger jar for containment. It was painstaking work but, by noon, in the larger of the two jars with its pierced lid, he had a dozen or more irate wasps. He was ready!

And at two that afternoon, he struck. He rang the front-door bell of Donal's presbytery, then immediately scuttled round the side of the building to the back door. As he expected, it was open, and he was quickly inside and concealed behind the inner door that opened from the hall into the kitchen.

"Yes? Yes? Is anyone there?" he heard the priest bellow. Seconds passed. "Feck!" The front door was slammed. The priest was returning to the kitchen. Donal was no sooner in the room than the man was upon him, clamping an impregnated cloth over Donal's mouth and nostrils. Within seconds the narcotic had done its work.

When Donal came to, he was bound to a chair at the kitchen table, upon which was a glass of *poteen* with a slightly cloudy appearance.

"'Ere, drink this," said a voice with slight foreign accent, and someone standing behind him leant over him and lifted the glass to his lips. Truth be told, however, Donal was glad of the liquid. He was significantly afraid. The *poteen* had a slightly strange taste, though, he noticed!

"Now," continued the same foreign voice, " you 'ave a key to the safe in the crypt. Where is it kept?"

"That is a secret I cannot reveal," said Donal, "to anyone, ever!"

"Really!" Seconds later a large, lidded jar containing wasps was placed on the table before him. "It is the work of a second, I assure you, to remove the lid."

From significant fear, Donal had lurched at once into gut-churning, knee-unhinging horror!

"No! No!" cried the priest. "Go into the pantry and lift up the short, loose floorboard on the right by the door. The key's there underneath it! Don't take the lid off that jar! Don't! Please! *Please!*"

"And was your mother a wanton whore?" asked the same, accented voice, now with a sibilant rasp of malicious mischief. The person reached from behind Donal and began to twist the lid of the jar.

"Yes! Yes!" screamed the priest.

"A dirty slut? A filthy slag?"

"Yes! She was! She was!"

"Mm!" The jar was left on the table unopened.

Fr. O'Hegarty heard footsteps retreating behind him towards the pantry. There were sounds of activity from within it, and then the footsteps approached him again. "Well, a key was indeed where you said one would be. This better be *the* one! The longer they're confined, the angrier those wasps will get, you know!"

For the man who called himself *Jacques Frelon*, administering the tranquiliser had been Plan B. But so great now was his contempt that he decided he would use his powers of hypnosis to serve this pitiable, little pastor as ill as he had served his sexton well. He waited till the physical signs were clear, and then again began to swing his watch…The man's voice became a soporific susurration, and within less than a minute, Donal was in deep hypnosis.

Two minutes later, Donal was, as it were, a loaded gun, and what would pull its trigger would be the words traditionally said at the end of the gospel. The sermon his congregation would receive on Sunday would begin … resoundingly!

At two that afternoon, even as the man who called himself *Jacques Frelon* was ringing the presbytery's front door bell, Stanley had another idea for his game of Calvary— the incorporation of a little tub into which would be put five screwed up pieces of paper. These would be torn along their perforations from sheets provided with the game. On the square just before the one called "Crucifixion" would be the words: "*Eli, Eli, lama sabachtani*'—what does it mean and who said it?" The player who landed on this square would have to pick a rolled-up piece of paper from the tub. Only one of the five pieces bore the correct answer: "'My God, My God, why have you forsaken me?'— Jesus on the Cross." By ten to four, Stanley was satisfied with some preliminary sketches of borders and motifs but had thought of only one possible wrong answer: "'Ali, Ali, I broke your jaw'—Ken Norton."

Stanley was already beginning to have second thoughts about this notion, but nonetheless, his gait was as jaunty as his heart was light when he set off for his weekly, contractual ritual.

As he approached the church, he saw that the door was open but that Fr. O'Hegarty was not outside waiting for him. Stanley ventured inside the church. He saw that the door to the crypt was also open and the stairwell lit. With mounting unease, he descended the spiral staircase, calling Fr. O'Hegarty's name, but response came there none. He froze in his tracks when he saw that the safe was open and that, in place of the chest that had been so successfully and secretly guarded for over eight hundred years, there was but a single key.

"Oh f…f…f…f…" he tried to exclaim.

Stanley bounded back up the stairs and rushed to the presbytery.

The tranquilliser administered to Donal was beginning to wear off, he was beginning to experience stiffness and cramp, and the lid on the wasp-filled jar still on the table in front of him looked less than tight the more he looked at it. His state of mind was deteriorating.

"Oh, Stanley! Stanley! I cannot tell you how pleased I am to see you," he gushed, with tears of gratitude glistening in his eyes after his sexton had freed him, poured him a brimming tumbler of *poteen* and taken the object of terror and hurled it far into the field behind the presbytery.

"F…F…F…Father, it's g…g…gone!"

It was several seconds before Donal realised that his sexton was not talking about the jar of wasps. "Oh, my God! Go on, Stanley, let me know the worst." Donal took stock of what Stanley had eventually told him, but which he should have realised would be the outcome of the afternoon's ordeal. "Oh! Jesus, Mary, and Joseph!" he murmured. "This couldn't be worse!"

Fleetingly, Stanley thought that Gangrene or advanced Malignant Melanoma could be slightly worse...though certainly this was *not* the moment to share this reflection with Fr. O'Hegarty, anyway, even if he could manage to! They were both approaching the very summit of the mountain called "Disaster."

The two of them sought further relief in two more brimming tumblers of *poteen.*

"Stanley," Donal said eventually, "this is entirely my fault.[10] I need a little time to take it in and decide what to do." He gulped down his tumbler of *poteen* like a dugong gulps down a single cranberry. "Stanley, bless you, and could you pour me another...and you must help yourself, too." The two men shared further moments of silent drinking, before Donal said, "I need to be on my own for a little while, Stanley, if you don't mind. I need time to think and pray." And leaning forward, he put his elbows on the table and cradled his chin in his hands, staring into some place only he could see.

Stanley looked at this broken figure, with the thinning, iron-grey hair he could imagine was once black and luxuriant; at the watery, bloodshot, blue eyes that he could imagine were once piercingly bright and

10   Devout Catholics receive guilt giros every week.

clear; at the bloated, veined face that he could imagine was once strikingly handsome; and he was wrung to his core by pity and his own sense of guilt.

"Of c…c…c…course."

As he walked down the hall, Stanley heard Fr. O'Hegarty distinctly murmur in a *poteen*-coarsened voice that he could imagine was once pure tenor: "My God, my God, why have you forsaken me?"

Stanley decided at once he would definitely abandon this addition to his game.

Chapter Seven

At six o'clock that same Friday evening, Fr. Donal O'Hegarty finally "bit the bullet." He went to his telephone and dialled the Vicar-General.

"Have you told anyone else—for instance, the police?" was the first icily curt question. "Good!" the same glacial voice continued when Donal said not. "At least you have managed to get one thing right. Tell *no one* else! Expect to see me first thing Sunday morning. Tell your sexton I wish to see him, too." The conversation had ended.

Canon Arnold Geldhard stood six feet, two inches tall in his bare feet. His frame was gaunt but seemed forever taut with energy he could barely contain. His face was long and skeletal and, behind glasses as thick as bottle-bottoms, was the suspicion of eyes that glittered with daunting acuity. Dressed always in a full-length, black cassock, this Vicar-General never simply entered a room—he swept into it. During cold weather, he always wore out-of-doors a full-length, hooded, black cape. He didn't simply walk along a path or pavement—he swept along them. The literary Donal had secretly dubbed him "The Lord Of The Nazgûl"[11] and dreaded him as if indeed he were.

---

11   I know that there will be readers who have never read or seen "The Lord Of The Rings" and have no intention of doing

The Talisman of Skerne   by Tom Carr

"Expect to see me first thing Sunday morning. Tell your sexton I wish to see him too."

so. For them, I will simply say that in the tale the "Nazgûl" or "Ringwraiths" are frightening entities and their leader, "The Lord Of The Nazgûl," particularly so!

At quarter to nine on Sunday morning, this person swept up the path to the front door of the presbytery, and on being ushered inside, swept along the hall and into Donal's living room. Stanley was already seated there. The burning ire that had brought his knee so recently into violent contact with the nadgers of the garden gnome salesman was now well nigh extinguished. He felt crushed.

Bowel-loosening seconds…as only such seconds can be…elapsed before the Vicar-General asked his questions.

He listened in inscrutable silence as first Donal and then Stanley related what had befallen them and gave him a description of the man who called himself *Jacques Frelon.* Donal in fact helped Stanley somewhat with his account, and for once, Stanley did not mind. It shortened the ordeal.

Finally, Canon Arnold Geldhard hissed his response and his voice was fell! "So, you chose to unravel the work of centuries, to undermine a Papal Edict itself, rather than put up with one or two insect stings, mm? *Craven oaf!*" he thundered. "And you!" he continued turning to Stanley. "Barely weeks into a well-paid and by no means onerous office, other than having the responsibility of guarding the chest, the paramount importance of which was made abundantly clear to you, what do *you* do? You invite a complete stranger into your house and allow him to hypnotise you! *Mindless moron!*" he bellowed.

This Vicar-General had a fundamental and passionate respect for the Old Testament God. Canon Arnold Geldhard was temperamentally uncomfortable with some relatively *modern* ideas. He did not accept that people should be presumed innocent until proven guilty. Man was, after all, fallen and weak. He had to look no further than the hapless duo facing him for present proof. Man was guilty! Perhaps only babes and the simple-minded might be considered innocent. Though not all the simple-minded! Certainly not these two! He was sure that confessions obtained under duress or torture were, for all the misgivings of *liberal* "do-gooders," valid nonetheless. Quite simply, for once in their miserable, venal lives, wrongdoers had encountered an effective inducement to tell the truth! And he could think of few more appropriate punishments to be meted out to the feckless pair now in his presence than fire and brimstone; unless, maybe, the rack, followed by burning or hanging, drawing and quartering. Crucifixion was certainly too good for them—it would put them on a par with their Saviour, which was an idea he found tantamount to blasphemous!

Nevertheless, after a brief glance at his watch, he said to Donal, "You have a Mass to say! Say it. *I* shall have a little more to say to both of you afterwards."

Donal and Stanley slunk in the wake of the terrible, cloaked figure to the church, into which the rest of its meagre congregation was shuffling.

Fr. O'Hegarty eventually began the Mass. When the moment arrived, he crossed the width of the altar to the lectern and began to read the day's gospel. Its message resonated poignantly: "Let he who has no sin cast the first stone." For even as he spoke, he was certain the Catholic hierarchy stood poised to bury him under a ton of rubble. This might be the last gospel he'd ever read to any congregation, and within the minute he could be delivering his very last sermon. When he finished the reading, he intoned as was customary, "This is the gospel of the Lord."

On cue, his miniscule congregation, now swelled by one, murmured, "Amen."

As it did so, it was as if a switch had tripped in his head. He looked at his paltry flock and then, despite the Vicar-General's dread presence, was unable to prevent himself from beginning his homily thus: "A vice both obscene and unsavoury, holds our very own Bishop in slavery. To maniacal howls, he rogers young owls, which he keeps in an underground aviary. In the name of the Father, and of the Son, and of the Holy Ghost." And he crossed himself.

Aware that he had, in fact, just said what he had just said, the doomed Donal thought frantically how on earth he could salvage even the least vestige of any priestly credibility. He resorted in final desperation to his literary training.

"No one has the slightest idea," he extemporised frantically, "why the 'Limerick'—the poetic form usually attributed to Edward Lear—should be named after a county in the west of Ireland, but there it is! Its rhyme scheme is A, A, B, B, A, and its metre quite precise: bum-titty-bum-titty-bum; bum-titty-bum-titty-bum; bum-titty-bum; bum-titty-bum; bum-titty-bum-titty-bum…"

Despite the more than usual interest his parishioners seemed to be taking in his sermon, he knew his ministry was now irrevocably wrecked by the treacherous iceberg with which it had been his recent, titanic misfortune to collide! Was there *poteen* enough left in his cellar to help him through this nightmare?

After Mass, Donal and Stanley again slunk in the wake of the "Nazgûl" back to the presbytery.

Installed again in Donal's living room, they awaited the Vicar-General's dread summation.

"A very interesting sermon," he finally hissed again, in those same fell and icy tones. "To add to the catalogue of your egregious blunders, I shall also point out in my report to the Bishop that I failed to see any religious or moral import in a quasi-literary discourse on a vulgar and obscene verse form that purported to be your homily—a desecration of the word that also made free reference to, among other things, bums and titties! I suggest you both start looking forthwith for a cheap removal firm and cheaper lodgings!" And with that he swept from their presence.

He would also include in his report, he had decided, the proposal that this dolt of an Irish priest—with a history of exposing himself to nuns and schoolgirls and of contemptible nervous debility—and who was now, in addition, clearly exhibiting signs of irrational, paranoid and delusional behaviour—no doubt fuelled by the liquor that was in clear evidence and probably illegal— should not simply be relieved of his parish but also be defrocked and thus cease to be a burden on any diocese unfortunate enough to have him anywhere in its midst!

With a glass of his illegal liquor in his hand, Donal looked forlornly at his rows of potatoes—not yet ready for harvesting—and wondered where his next year's supply of *poteen* would come from.

Stanley—his stutter once again severe—could not bring himself to make his customary Sunday evening visit to the pub. He looked woefully at his newly acquired pieces of furniture, and supposed they would have to be returned. How else now was he going to pay off his Barclaycard debt? So Cheryl would never see them, or any of the other things he had so wanted to show her. Indeed, would *he* ever see Cheryl again?

Chapter Eight

Though, as it turned out, the man who called himself *Jacques Frelon* need not have been so circumspect; nonetheless, he had anticipated a possible attempt to try and intercept him at one of the channel ports. Which was why he had boarded an overnight ferry from Tynemouth to Rotterdam on the very same afternoon that he had seized the chest.

The crossing had been calm, the food and wine pleasant, and his cabin comfortable. In it, he had had time to carefully inspect the spoils of his machinations. All was as he had hoped! Afterwards he slept well.

The passengers were roused the following morning in four languages. First a lilting Dutch voice asked: "*Uw aandacht, alstublieft, aub kunnen de passagiers hun cabines verlaten...*" Next, a calm English voice politely enjoined: "Your attention, please. Would passengers kindly leave their cabins…" Thirdly, came the mellifluous French request: "*Votre attention, s'il vous plait. Les passagers sont priés de quitter leurs cabines…*" And then finally: "*Achtung, bitte…*" At once, all on board were pouring into the corridors.

And of course among them was the man who called himself *Jacques Frelon*. Once on dry land, he would set in motion, by means of a single 'phone call to some so-called accomplices, a chain of events which could prove very interesting. But he alone knew these would be a mere smoke screen; he alone knew the greater purpose that would be served by his acquisition of the chest. He had also taken other necessary steps that were now very close to fruition, too. Within perhaps just over a week, all would coalesce, and his everlasting glory would be assured! For the Master he served would certainly reward him greatly for this work!

Again, to be circumspect, but also to play the tourist for a few days longer, he meandered through Holland, Belgium, Germany, and Luxembourg before re-entering France just north of Metz and then heading southwest to the town where he presently resided.

His Eminence Padraig Finbar O'Flagherty-Ahearn sat at the Chippendale desk in his sumptuous, Dublin office and pondered the two pieces of information he had just received. His thoughts were complex, and he decided not to do anything hasty. He would let his ideas gestate over a twenty-four-hour period before he took any action.

He had just learned of the disappearance of the abominable artefact from the church in Grimdon Lea, and he had also just received very disturbing, related information from the Vatican itself.

The Cardinal had a particular fondness for Irish coffee, properly percolated from fine, ground Brazilian beans and laced with a generous measure of Dublin's own Jamesons. Now was a good time to have one. It would clarify his thinking. A glassful was summoned immediately.

A minute or two after drinking it, Padraig Finbar O'Flagherty-Ahearn reflected on the decision he had initially taken and told himself that it was good. It was right he should make *no* decision today. He would make a decision tomorrow. And he decided that his decision not to make a decision today was, in fact, decidedly, one of the best decisions he had ever made. So he decided he would have another Irish coffee to celebrate this sage decision. When he took his first sip from his second glass he decided this decision, too, was decidedly a good one!

The following day, however, the Cardinal took decisive action. He began by booking a flight to Teesside Airport on a prestigious Irish airline and arranging a rendezvous in a convent in Darlington with the Bishop of Hexham and Newcastle and his Vicar-General. Then he made a 'phone call to the south of France. From this, he learned that the person he wished to speak to was, in fact, aestivating[12] in the north of England, which was serendipity indeed. He 'phoned the number he had just been given and was shortly in contact with the person he sought. Within half a minute, he had arranged for another, separate meeting to take place in the same location.

"I do appreciate that you have heeded my advice and taken no steps in the matter of our own poor Fr. O'Hegarty and his unhappy sexton," said the Cardinal to the Bishop. "Thank you. There are complicated,

---

12   This is *not* a mortal sin!

political ramifications to this chain of events—which I will explain to you shortly—which make it expedient that nothing should draw the attention of unwanted, prying eyes to them. That all appears as it should be in Grimdon Lea is very much for the best."

Seated beside his Bishop, the Vicar-General seethed with silent anger. He could not understand why this man should be meddling in the affairs of a diocese so far removed from his own. Why was he so interested in the matter? It couldn't be because of the involvement of that insignificant apology for a priest, O'Hegarty, surely? Canon Arnold Geldhard's present position was, indeed, not so far from that of a "Nazgul" who had suddenly seen "Sauron"[13] himself deprive him of his appointed prey. Behind the bottle-bottom lenses, the Vicar-General's eyes glittered with ire, and Cardinal Padraig Finbar O'Flagherty-Ahearn became aware of them.

"I suggest you extend some pity to those two unfortunates, Canon," said the Cardinal, turning towards him. "This so-called *Jacques Frelon* is known to us, and believe you me, he is an enemy against whom even you would not have fared well!"

Sunday had passed into Monday, Monday into Tuesday, and Tuesday into Wednesday and still, for Donal and Stanley, the anticipated, dreaded axe had

13   For the same non-aficionados, "Sauron" is the eponymous, evil "Lord Of The Rings" and the nine "Nazgul" his most terrible servants. If you are open to the idea, and can wangle six months paid leave, you might enjoy the book.

not fallen. Donal had started taking pleasure again in his Fielding and had resumed watering his potatoes. Stanley had rediscovered some relish in his work on "Calvary," had begun affectionately patting his newly acquired furniture, and finally decided that on Thursday evening, he would venture again to the pub. So he *would* see the lovely Cheryl once more—and even if it was just the once more, he would contrive, come hell or high water, to make the encounter special, stammer or no stammer!

The glorious summer continued unabated. Stanley's heart was close to light when he arrived at the lane's end, opposite The Golden Cock. And at that moment, his luck took a further upturn. One of two youths who happened to be standing at the side of the lane asked him, "Who are you looking at?"

"S…s…s…sorry?"

"S…s…s…" began the youth, smirking horribly at his companion.

It took Stanley just one bound to reach his antagonist and head-butt him viciously, felling him to the ground. He turned with raised fists but the other youth had already taken to his heels. "Wanker!" Stanley bellowed at his retreating back.

"Oh, hello," said Cheryl with her knee-weakening, scrotum-tightening smile. "I missed you on Sunday night. I wanted to thank you for sorting out that scumbag who was pestering me last week. I don't know exactly what you did to him, but whatever it was, it did the trick. I didn't get another peep out of him for the rest of the time he was here. I really appreciate it. Thanks again."

"My pleasure," said Stanley.

"Mm!" Cheryl continued, " your...you know...it's better!"

"Stammer," said Stanley. "Yes, I know. That other bloke you thought was quite creepy actually helped me quite a bit," Stanley said, not wholly untruthfully, "and then one or two other things have helped, as well. It comes and goes..." Stanley pressed home his advantage. "Do you have a night off?"

"Yes, Wednesday."

"Could I take you out somewhere, then, next Wednesday?"

Due to the response he received, Stanley's knees had never felt weaker nor his scrotum so taut!

⚜

"Welcome, old friend," said Cardinal Padraig Finbar O'Flaherty-Ahearn, extending his hand, "so nice to see you again, so good of you to come."

His tall, elegantly dressed guest shook his hand but maintained a cool aplomb. Though they had been acquaintances for a long time and had shared some harrowing experiences, a bond of true, deep friendship did not exist between them, and both knew it. The Cardinal obviously wanted something of some importance, to offer so effusive a greeting. However, the refined, civilised recipient betrayed nothing of these thoughts in his noble countenance, as he made *his* greetings. He would keep an open mind.

Padraig Finbar O'Flagherty-Ahearn's charm offensive continued—brandy and cigars were produced. But, finally, the Cardinal began his narrative, which culminated in his request. His guest had listened with increasingly grave interest and then finally made his response.

"What you have told me is disturbing. I take it very seriously. Would you allow me a little time for reflection and for discussion…for I have guests arriving tomorrow who could be of some assistance in this…indeed you already know them…"

The Cardinal could do no other than acquiesce. "Thank you. How long do you need?"

"I shall give you my reply on Sunday."

"Thank you."

"Mm!" murmured his guest in afterthought. "*Jacques Frelon*! I wonder at which point this individual settled upon this alias? Given his knowledge of which weakness to exploit in the priest, it suggests a malicious sense of irony."

"How so?"

"How so? '*Frelon*' is the French for 'hornet.'"

Just prior to the theft of the chest and its contents, the morale of The Four Horsemen Of The Apocalypse had for some time been, on average, average. "War" had seen, during the year, the so-called "Dirty Wars" in Argentina, the London "Gang Wars," and there were already rumours of "Star Wars." "Conquest" had seen the launch of "Conquest Of The Amazon" by John Russell Fearn and the board game "Galactic Conquest." "Famine" was comforting himself with junk food. Though things globally were no better than the previous year, neither had they had got any worse! Damn Oxfam and the United Nations! Only "Death" seemed content. He had got himself one of these new-fangled computers and was using something called a "spreadsheet" to keep a tally. "You know," he would remark smugly, from time to time, as he entered data, during breaks from whetting his scythe, "there are people dying today who've never died before!" He was seriously irritating his three co-workers. But actually, all four of them would be more than pleased if Armageddon arrived pretty soon. They'd been hanging around waiting for it, for what seemed like an eternity!

Then word reached them that the chest had been stolen. In the past, the chest's infamous contents, they knew, had been put to quite frivolous use. But knowledge of who now held the chest stirred all four of them strangely. This person surely knew the real, terrible power of the things he had in his possession. And for what other reason would he have stolen these things but to unleash their might? Very shortly, indeed, the four of them might finally get to see some seriously spectacular action! "Nee hah!" they each in turn whooped with glee, as they gave their horses their daily gallop round the exercise paddock.

PART TWO

Chapter Nine

The *Duc de Cornsai-Tantobé* lifted between the forefinger and thumb of his long, aristocratic, well-manicured right hand the cork he had just prised from the bottle of 1963 *Ricardo Montalaban* port, a rare *gento–puskàs cépage*, and held it to his distinguished, well-coiffured nostrils, which opened into his noble, aquiline nose.

"Mmm!" he murmured approvingly, in that deep, resonant baritone that was his alone: "it is not corked..." adding; "...*heureusement!*" in an accent so *classique* that his two guests imagined themselves momentarily transported from the *Duc's* Yorkshire retreat of "Throstlenest Hall" to "*la rive gauche.*"

He poured a little of the dark, rich liquid into a new, exquisite, ellipsoid, cut-glass goblet, which bore, by means of subtle etching, his family emblem, swirled the wine expertly, first to see its "*couleur*" then test its "*bouquet,*" before taking a "*bouchée,*" which he savoured with expert, buccal dexterity. Finally, he swallowed and announced to his two old friends: "I think you will appreciate this; it is...sardonic but not cynical!"

His guests voiced their thanks as their exquisite, ellipsoid, cut-glass goblets were charged. These vessels also bore, by means of subtle etching, the *Duc's* family emblem; from the same set, both men had simultaneously yet independently deduced with peerless percipience!

As they took their first sips, the *Duc* looked at his two old friends and a pang of anxiety furrowed his distinguished brow. "Could I? Should I?"

They had experienced, and survived, so many dangers together. They had even emerged, though not wholly unscathed, from Woodstock; their mission there, surveillance on behalf of the American government. They had blended into the crowd in their ridiculous, patchouli-impregnated, Indian print kaftans, ever vigilant for and reporting on anything *seriously* anti-establishment! So they had had to endure the sacrilegious abuse of that exquisite voice—Joan Baez peddling pinko-liberal claptrap; and that weasel-faced, nasal yid whining about the times a-changing! All grist to the mill of the Forces Of Darkness!

So, for the undertaking that had been requested of him, the *Duc* could not think of two more stalwart or dependable allies. But could he ask them to face one more peril? For he knew if he did, they would not refuse!

He looked at them surreptitiously and a deep, but wholly chaste, love welled in his noble breast. No! He could not! The Holy See would have to look elsewhere!

As if divining his thoughts, *Hatch Beauchamp*, his huge American friend, spoke. His lazy, New Orleans drawl belied an incisive intellect. A Harvard graduate in Astro-physics, he had also been considered the only boxer of his generation capable of beating *Mohammed Ali* in his prime, but the two were never destined to meet in the ring, *Hatch* because he had gone to fight in Vietnam, the craven black because he had refused to do so...

"So, *Théo*"—*Hatch* always used the diminutive of the *Duc's prénom*—"yaw ain't foolin' nawbody nawhow. What yaw got thar up that old sleeve o' yourn, yaw wily raccoon?"

"In Russia, also is there zis saying about sleefes. The conspirator he vears them long and baggy…to hide away his secrets…*Hatch* and I know you haf one. Vhen vill you take it out from up your sleef, *Mon Cher Théodore?*"

Alexandrov Slivovitch Romanov, indeed related to that royal and tragic lineage, and as great a contrast to his American friend imaginable, looked quizzically with his one eye at the *Duc.* A prestigious Soviet biochemist, his injuries had been sustained while keeping at bay a pod of ravening narwhals till all his comrades from the ill-fated cetacean study ship, *Skromsk,* had safely reached the haven of an arctic ice flow. Wounds and frostbite had taken their toll! Formerly a tenth Dan in jujitsu, despite his gracile, diminutive frame, he now had other means of self-defence of his own devising. The elegant cedar-wood cane on which, perforce, he now had to lean had at its lower end a botulinum-impregated stiletto released by a turn of its embossed, silver knob, which if tilted and pressed, would also release from an eyelet just beneath it a jet of concentrated hydrofluoric acid! The sable glove he always wore on his right hand to hide his two missing fingers was lined with a hydrofluorocarbon polymer of his own invention, as self-protection against that most corrosive of chemicals.

The official silence about and indifference to the fate of the ship and its crew—you will find no reference to it anywhere[14]—had led *Alexandrov Slivovitch* to defect at the first opportunity…and it had been the *Duc* who had provided that opportunity during their first adventure together.[15]

"Yes, indeed. I do have something up my sleeve… but I need more time to reflect…thank you so much, both of you, for…helping me focus my thoughts…"

"Ve are bored! *Hatch* and I haf both decided zis, yes…you vant us to participate in an…adventure…how you say zis, *Hatch*?"

"Whatever it is, we're up for…whatever it is…yes, indeedy!"

"I did not invite you here because I had an 'adventure' in mind, *mes amis*; it just happens that the possibility of one has arisen…but it is because of my love for you both that, at the eleventh hour, I have had sudden doubts… but as always you …what is that quaint, Anglo-Saxon seafaring phrase…if we are in their little island we are permitted a little borrowing, *non*? 'You have taken the wind out of my sails'. *Mais comme d'habitude*."

Again, it was as if the other two had been instantly transported, but this time to the luminous *paysage* of *Languedoc* and the *Duc's* ancestral home, *Le Château du Prat Ragé*…

"I suspect a sea-change…forgive me, the nautical metaphors become *un peu de trop*, I fear…but let me sleep on it…we will talk frankly over breakfast. Your usual rooms await you. Now, if you permit, I will retire… help yourselves to whatever you want…*faites commes chez*

---

14   Except here.
15   See *Satan's Todger* by the same author.

vous. And also as the Zulus[16] say, '*ulalani kamnandi*' ... sleep well...*à demain...*"

But the *Duc* did not retire at once to his bedroom. Unbeknown to his friends, he had a nightly check to make, which now led him along chandeliered corridors to the farthermost reaches of the baronial edifice, for indeed, such it was. Originally built by the *De Monteforts*, it had been given to the *Duc's* family as recompense for their help in the wholesale massacre of the inhabitants of *Béziers* in 1209. No doubt seen as a mere *bagatelle* to the *De Monteforts*, this rambling, limestone pile in a cold, remote and barbarous land, it was held nevertheless in great affection by the *Duc*, his favourite retreat from the merciless cauldron of the *Languedocian* summer.

Located in a small, old outhouse personally re-designed by the *Duc*, heated and humidified by a separate generator so no power cut would ever jeopardise his secret *passe-temps*, this was probably the only private slothery in the whole of the United Kingdom. *Tristan* and *Iseult*, the *Duc's* two three-toed sloths, hung in peaceful slumber from separate branches of the two secropia trees burgeoning there. The fur of each animal was rich with moss and the moths browsed it avidly. All were in prime condition. The *Duc* expected the two eventually to breed, but they were sloths, they took their time. He checked the temperature and humidity gauges, cast an

---

16   To explain the *Duc's* fluency in Zulu, see "The Impis of Beelzebub," also by the same author.

affectionate, parting glance at the somnolent duo, and withdrew, gently closing the door behind him.

Between the slothery and his bedroom, the *Duc* had made his decision. And his qualms were now wholly replaced by a mounting excitement. He and his two friends were again about to unravel a mystery, again to face unknown foes and daunting obstacles, all so the world would remain a safer place.

He took from the polished, olivewood table beside his caste-iron, four poster bed, bedecked with delicate, taupe, linen bed sheets and drapes, the new exquisite, ellipsoid, cut-glass decanter, which bore by means of subtle etching his family emblem and poured into the equally new, exquisite, ellipsoid, cut-glass brandy glass which also bore by means of subtle etching his family emblem—the two *objets d'art* (for indeed they merited this term) were now always at his bedside—a nightcap of vintage *Renier-Renato cognac.*

As he savoured the smooth, heady liqueur, he felt also an expanding contentment. Against all previous expectation, he knew now that he would sleep well!

Chapter Ten

Raised to appreciate the delicacies of *la cuisine française*, such as *pâté de foie gras* (paste of fatty liver) and *rillettes de boeuf* (pulped bullock's innards), it had taken the *Duc* some time to educate his palate to the breakfasts Flora, his Scottish housekeeper, took such delight in offering to him and his guests in Throstlenest Hall: black pudding (*sang de porc coagulé*), chitterlings (*estomac de vache haché*), scrambled eggs (*oeufs brouillés en matière graisse*), haggis (*blague écossaise*), and royal porridge (*bouillie d'avoine au whisky*).

It was in the course of such a breakfast the following morning that the *Duc* related to his two guests the gist of his meeting earlier that week with His Eminence Padraig Finbar O'Flagherty-Ahearn—telling them only what was germane to the proposed mission. Much else related personally only to the *Duc* and the Prelate.

The two were old acquaintances; the *Duc* could not say friends; a distance separated them, on the one hand because of the Cleric's exalted position in the Church; on the other hand because, despite the Irishman's exalted ecclesiastical position, both knew he was much lesser an Adept than the *Duc*! The Cardinal had flown from Dublin to Teesside, using a prestigious Irish airline and had met with the *Duc* in a Catholic convent in Darlington. The *Duc* had chosen to travel the fifty or so miles there from Throstlenest Hall unobtrusively, eschewing the Bentley for his much less ostentatious Jaguar.

As always, his *chauffeur* had made excellent time. Being French, he had no compunction ignoring speed restrictions, and had mastery of an intimidating use of the horn. The *chauffeur's* family had been linked to the *Duc's* as underlings for over a century. But *Jean Le Taureau* owed the *Duc* a particular loyalty. He had returned a day earlier than expected from his last tour of service in the French Foreign Legion to find his wife spraddled beneath the bucking body of her paramour, the manager of the local branch of *Crédit Agricole*. If she had chosen a rugby player, perhaps he might have reacted with more circumspection...but a banker![17]

He had killed them both on the spot. As this was *une crime passionelle* and also *la tramontane* wind had been blowing infuriatingly all day, under French law he had a good chance of getting away with a small fine. However, such an outcome still necessitated paying for a good lawyer and the means to pay the fine. The good *Duc* had provided both. Now there was nothing *Jean Le Taureau* would not do for his benefactor.

As the *Duc* got out of the Jaguar, *Jean* asked, "When should I expect to pick you up, *Seigneur?*"

"I have no idea how long this will take, I'm afraid... just be here when I come out."

"*Bien sûr.*"

Fortunately—*Jean Le Taureau* quickly divined—as there were no parking restrictions in the locality where the *Duc* had issued this instruction, "being there" when

---

17   The southern French also have a variant of the cockney "*argot rimant.*"

the *Duc* came out would pose no problem whatsoever… however piffling he had ever found such problems to be, even in Paris or London.

As to what followed, the *Duc, Jean* decided, would receive only an edited version. Particularly relaxed as he now was with this lack of a problem, *Jean Le Taureau* got out of the car, crossed the road to the shade of a tree, and lit up a *Gauloise*. One minute later, he saw two spotty youths approaching the car on the opposite pavement. After a brief, smirking exchange, one of them reached down into the grass verge, picked up something, and did something to the far side of the car. *Jean* had remained unnoticed and allowed thirty seconds for their laughing departure. He then re-crossed the road to discover a long scratch gouged into the paintwork of the Jaguar. Though at once seized by a murderous rage, *Jean Le Taureau* had nonetheless learned circumspection. A quick scan of the street revealed lots more trees, shade, and more happily, no other people or traffic. Silently, for so big a man, he padded after them and, as luck would have it, reached them at the secluded entrance to a large, private house. With pantherine suddenness, he seized them both, banged their heads together violently and dragged their unconscious bodies into the shaded grounds. A karate chop to the larynx dispatched them both. He left the cadavers in a dark corner of the garden. It would probably be some time before they were discovered. There had been no witnesses. He had worn his chauffeur's gloves throughout. *Fait accompli!* He returned to the shade of his tree and enjoyed a second *Gauloise*. He decided to swig a large, celebratory *bouchée* of *calvados* from his hip flask too.

cW✵

While this wholly appropriate act of natural justice had unfurled, another drama of a different sort had played out between the *Duc* and the Cardinal, the gist of which *Théodore de Cornsai-Tantobé* was now imparting to his two guests.

"Let me ask you, *mes amis*, have you ever heard of the 'Talisman of Skerne?'"

His friends both shook their heads.

"Nor had I till my meeting with the Cardinal last week. 'Skerne,' it would appear, posed as a Christian missionary in the twelfth century and sought out areas of the northeast of England, which had been untouched by the influence of Cuthbert or Bede—places like 'No Place,' 'Pity Me,' and 'Wallish Walls'…"

The *Duc* saw his friends' incredulous expressions.

"Let me assure you, *mes amis*, these places existed… exist even to this day…but let me continue…Skerne, it seems, had his own very personal version of Christianity… He was in possession of a 'Talisman'—a golden phallus of unknown origin and antiquity—that he claimed conferred on him, its keeper designate, through the power of the Holy Ghost, the ability to cure barrenness. He was, he said, merely the earthly intermediary of The Paraclete, his own flesh and blood phallus the corporeal means by which the Third Person of the Holy Trinity could enter the bodies of infertile women to work his miracles.[18]

---

18   This is thought by many reputable historians of music to be the inspiration for Gershwin's lyric: "Nice work if you can get it, and you can get it if you try"…

The Talisman of Skerne   by Tom Carr

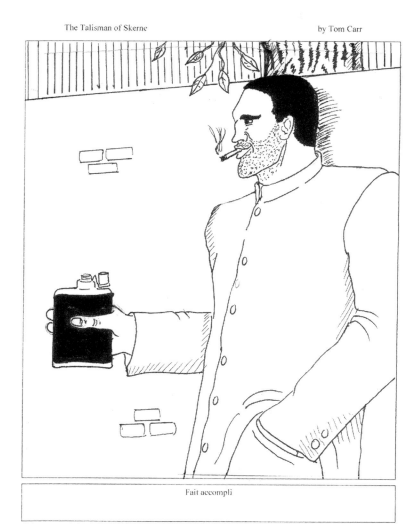

Fait accompli

"*De toute façon*,"—for both his listeners there was again another brief *soupçon* of somewhere in France— "when word reached the Pope of the real nature of Skerne's missionary position, he was excommunicated immediately for heresy and, not long afterwards, on learning this, a mob of irate, local men seized him and burnt him at the stake. A chest, in which Skerne kept his 'Talisman' together with documents which supposedly verified its provenance and authenticity, and also described various rites associated with its powers, was immediately seized by the local Bishop and removed to a secure and undisclosed location.

"However, discredited as Skerne was by Holy Mother church, the allure of his 'Talisman' continued and even grew. In this century, the Church has become aware of a secret society that sees Skerne as an emancipator of women well ahead of his time, a martyr to medieval ignorance and superstition. This sect has been actively seeking to discover the location of Skerne's chest and its contents for some time."

The *Duc* forked another morsel of black pudding into his noble, perfectly proportioned mouth, savoured its subtle, haematic taste, and allowed his friends a few moments to assimilate what he had said.

Then he continued: "The location of the 'Talisman' has been known to only a handful of people throughout the ages, and it has been extremely well guarded...but, *mes amis*, unbelievably, Skerne's chest and its contents have disappeared...and it turns out this could have serious consequences...because of the actual intentions of the sect…which have been conveyed in a written message to the Holy See itself just last week…"

The *Duc* was again silent to let this further information be assimilated by his two friends. As they did so, he carefully brushed unseemly, black crumbs from the delicate, taupe, linen tablecloth covering the highly polished, olive wood table at which they had breakfasted.

Chapter Eleven

The *Duc* had ceased his narrative—though there was still more to say—as they had ceased their breakfast...so nice was his sense of timing.

He would give them time to reflect. He had then proposed they should resume over lunch. In the meantime—if they would excuse him—he had other matters that, *hélas*, demanded his attention; but he felt sure, *n'est-ce pas*, that the two of them would have things to do, too?

His two friends assured him warmly that this *délicatesse* was as always greatly appreciated.

Hatch returned to his room to do his daily two hundred sit-ups, one hundred press-ups, and nine neck and jaw-strengthening, whole-body lifts, gripping solely with his teeth the strong, nylon cord he had slung over his door and tied to the banister beyond it. That elusive tenth heave seemed tantalisingly closer. Maybe tomorrow, if he breakfasted more lightly...Then he showered, dressed casually in crocodile skin boots over yellow, cotton socks, terracotta chinos, and an olive-green, silk shirt, and sat down to relax with some light reading—*Dream and Symbol in Jungian Psychology*...What refreshing, welcome relief from the complexities of electron-positron interactions...

Meanwhile, *Alexandrov Slivovitch* had retired to his room to work some more on the chemical formula of a complex toxin of his own devising, which he felt was so close now to realisation…a substance so lethal, it would kill instantly, yet metabolise at once to carbon dioxide and water, the body's natural waste products, so as to render it completely without trace. He knew this was, at once, an intellectual challenge *and* a vicarious purging of rage, as he envisioned the whole of the *Politburo* succumbing to the lacing of their brimming, privileged glasses of premium vodka with his wholly undetectable poison! Indeed, he had in mind someone he knew in the Soviet Union who might do such a thing! *Alexandrov Slivovitch* had felt no need to change from his collarless, white, cotton, belted smock and brown, billowing, serge trousers, tucked into saïga-hide, calf-length boots.

To assuage the *Duc's* dismay, *Jean Le Taureau* had informed him that the piece of minor damage to the nearside bodywork of the Jaguar was inexplicable but that the repair was being effected. He hoped the *Duc* would not be deranged by this, or by the fact that they would, for a day or two, be obliged to employ uniquely the Bentley!

As always, the *Duc* felt the satisfaction of knowing how well he had chosen personnel who could deal so efficiently with such petty inconveniences.

The *Duc* had checked on *Tristan* and *Iseult*, as he always did mid morning. They were sleeping peacefully…and then the *Duc* made a crucial telephone call…

Later, the *Duc* suggested to his friends that they dine just after noon at The Dingleberry Arms—in effect, his local pub—a charming, sixteenth-century warren of a building, situated in the heart of the nearest village,

Wangthwaite. The pub served wholesome, traditional Yorkshire fare and a potent brew, known in the locality as "Badger's Arse."

The *Duc* chose skewered squirrel with mashed swede and potato—how his palate had diversified! *Hatch* picked goat and mushroom pie with parsnips, sprouts, and potatoes cooked in stout; and *Alexandrov Slivovitch* selected a thrush, cabbage, and beetroot casserole. They all decided it essential to wash down their meal with local ale.

"*Bon appétit*," said the *Duc*. Again for his friends, there was that instant transportation to somewhere in France, but this time, inexplicably for *Hatch*, also the evocation of a meeting with an elfin girl in a French *restaurant*. The encounter had lasted but a short time but had remained ever since in his memory. It had been in the town of *Nevers* on a Sunday…the last Sunday of a particularly good September, just last year, when he had decided to drive down from Paris to the *Languedoc* in leisurely fashion for his annual week's holiday with the *Duc* and *Alexandrov Slivovitch*. She and *Hatch* had spoken for a good half-hour, seated at adjoining tables, before she too had said, "*Bon appétit*" at the arrival of his *moules frites*. Then she had left, but with a parting, lingering glance that haunted him to this day…*Marie Laverge… mais bien sûr*, he would remember her name…

He had wondered afterwards if it had been mere wishful thinking, and that, in fact, he had *not* seen her again on his return to Paris for his flight home. It was just that, for a while, he saw her face in every crowd… maybe it was the price of love? Could it indeed be that?

He had stayed overnight in the beautiful valley of *La Loire*. The memories tumbled pell-mell...*Chinon*... harvest moon...her lissom form on the bridge...even a glance of knowing recognition...then gone. Had he imagined it? He did not know!

The authoritive, deep, resonant baritone that was the *Duc's* alone brought *Hatch* out of his reverie.

The *Duc* had reserved the tiny room, which seated only three, in which only the three of them were now seated so that the three of them would be the only ones to hear what was to be said. *Jean Le Taureau* meanwhile was enjoying the balmy English summer[19] in the beer garden, eating a thirty-two ounce T-bone steak with chips, also accompanied by the local ale, and renewing his acquaintance with Betty the barmaid, who found his French accent so irresistible that, when on his visits here, he proposed to her some late-night activity; she never resisted.

"Let me continue from where I left off this morning," the *Duc* had begun. "I do not need to tell you that we live in an increasingly secular age...indeed you have seen this and its results in your own country, *n'est-ce pas, mon cher Alexandrov?* As the Cardinal pointed out to me, both the number of priests Our Holy Mother church recruits and the number of believers diminishes...that our cherished holy institutions seem increasingly fragile... *Eh bien*, it seems that another power was attributed to Skerne's 'Talisman.' His Eminence would not divulge to me its nature; but he assured me it is of a different order to the risible, carnal chicanery of a medieval trickster. He tells me it is deeply blasphemous and, as such, a

---

19   Occasionally there is one!

weapon that would be greatly welcomed by the Powers of Darkness that assail the Church.

"The sect is effectively blackmailing His Holiness himself. It wants a restitution of Skerne's 'good name' and even a *bona fide* investigation into his possible canonisation. Otherwise, it will reveal to the world's media the exact nature of this blasphemy with the 'evidence' that supports it. The consequences, in the Cardinal's view, could be grave. First, many may take the blasphemy as 'gospel' and claim it even further undermines the legitimacy of the Church, which will undoubtedly lessen even more the numbers of the faithful...those whose faith is not so robust in the first place...those who were considering baptism but could be dissuaded...Furthermore, it could involve the Church in a lengthy, costly and difficult refutation of the blasphemy, which it can ill afford at this time, and the success of which it could not wholly guarantee, for its numerous enemies would mount counter argument after counter argument to continuing, damaging effect!

"*Apparemment,* I also learned, this is not the first time in recent years that the Church has had to deal with such a crisis! Not that long ago, an obscure French *curé* claimed he had found 'evidence' that Jesus had not died but recovered from His Ordeal on the Cross, left the Holy Land, and married Mary Magdalen...*Sacrebleu,* what sort of *imbécile* could possibly find this *folie* more plausible than Christ's death, resurrection, and ascension into heaven? *Mais heureusement,* this nonsense gained no ground."

The *Duc* suddenly slapped his noble forehead with the palm of his slender, aristocratic hand. "*Ma foi,*" he cried, "the decommissioning of the Inquisition, the suspension of the laws against blasphemy, the rise of Amnesty International...does this represent *vraiment du progrès?*"

Such an outburst was all the more eloquent for being so rare.

But the *Duc* had as quickly regained composure. "Our mission, should we accept it," he said, "is to take steps to ensure this latest *bêtise* gains no currency either..."

The arrival of Betty to check on the progress of their meal cut the *Duc* short.

"Five more minutes, Betty, please...and then perhaps some coffee and *cognac?*"

Though his accent was even more exquisitely French than his *chauffeur's*, and the tall, aristocratic *Duc* still a strikingly handsome man, despite being somewhat older, he was also sufficiently modest to grant that the flush already suffusing Betty's comely face, swan-like neck, and partly exposed, delectable bosom, *en plus* the glorious state of erection of the nipples thrusting against her white, frilly, diaphanous cotton blouse beneath, which she clearly wore no bra[20], surely arose from whatever *Jean Le Taureau* had just said to her.

"There is still more," announced the *Duc* when, again, there were only the three of them in the room. "*Mais à plus tard.* Let us each enjoy the rest of the meal and our *petit digestif.*"

---

20   Certain English readers may consider the *Duc* somewhat prurient. If so, I would simply caution, do not forget that the *Duc* is French. Indeed, the *Duc* himself would be quite content to have engraved on his tombstone, like Thomas Hardy: "He was a man who noticed such things." But then most men notice such things!

The Talisman of Skerne   by Tom Carr

The *Duc*... like most men... noticed such things!

Chapter Twelve

It was a particularly sunny August across the whole of France, and, of course, being August, the whole of France was therefore enjoying *des bonnes vacances*.

Marie Laverge awoke to her first morning in her mother's *appartement* in *Nevers*. She had just spent a week with her father, *Joachim*, in *Chinon*. He had taken her out yesterday and bought her a new jumper, cardigan, scarf, and woollen skirt—tomorrow would be the *quinze août* and, therefore, inevitably, the weather would change abruptly. She had forgotten to consider this when she had packed, the blazing sun of *Montpelier*—where she worked as a medical researcher—seemed eternal.

Anne Laverge was already in the long room that was lounge, diner, and kitchen, though still in her tasteful, coordinated, mauve negligée, bra, and culottes, her almond eyes bright with anticipation of the promise of the day, when her daughter appeared. *Marie* was still in her tasteful, coordinated, cérise negligée, bra, and culottes, her almond eyes still half-glazed with sleep.

Mother and daughter could be taken for sisters, were it not for the slight tinge of grey that appeared in *Anne's* hair, which unlike *Marie,* she wore very short— and the fading of that youthful voluptuousness that still suffused *Marie's* shoulders, arms, breasts, buttocks, thighs, and calves—so that sometimes the mother was now called "handsome" rather than "beautiful," though beautiful indeed she still was, as was voluptuously so her daughter!

Both had the same elfin face, pert, rose-bud lips, straight, perfectly proportioned nose, and dark, liquid eyes that men might drown in…but also figures so lissom and slender, stomachs and abdomens so exquisitely flat that it remains to this day an enigma why no one has ever seen either of them on the front cover of *Vogue*.

"Breakfast, *Ma Petite?*" enquired *Anne*. At her daughter's nod of assent, *Anne* immediately turned on the oven and placed in it a tray laden with *croissants* and *pains au chocolat*. As these were heating, *Marie* made her way to the table that was already laid and where nestled a very large bowl heaving with apples, bananas, figs, grapes, nectarines, oranges, peaches, pears, and quince. ("Ah!" thought *Marie* immediately, "so that is why Maman has put out *les cuillères runcibles!*") From the fridge *Anne* brought tubs of natural yoghurt.

After they had devoured all of this splendid fare, *and* the *croissants* and *pains au chocolat*, washed down with a bowl of *café crème*, *Anne* announced that she had some articles to collect from the local library, which she had commissioned from elsewhere, part of a little, historical-research project she had begun. She proposed a rendezvous for lunch at midday in their favourite restaurant.

Marie was pleased to have some time to herself to read—she already was halfway through *Schrödinger and His Cat—Quantum Reality Explained* and was eager to continue…

VOGUE

Mère et Fille

Belles de tous les jours

Anne et Marie Laverge

It remains to this day an enigma why this has never happened…

She and her mother arrived at "*Le Cul de Blaireau*" almost simultaneously at five past twelve. Already, the restaurant was filling...but *Anne* and *Marie* had reserved a table...*heureusement*...

Opposite them at three tables set side by side were numerous members of the local police and fire service, already savouring their first *Ricard*s. It is a little appreciated aspect of French life, but important, nonetheless, that so sacrosanct is the two-hour lunch break that murderers, thieves, and arsonists will not give it up either. Therefore, the agencies of law enforcement and fire protection can almost always be assured of a long, relaxed, carefree, midday meal.

An unfamiliar waiter—a summer temp, maybe—approached *Anne* and *Marie*, leering salaciously at them both and addressed them in an exaggeratedly suggestive tone: "*Vous désirez?*" he growled, all the while rubbing the front of his trousers to suggest he possessed a "weapon" of such wondrous potency both of them would remain forever in his debt if they took the opportunity to sample it. (Incredibly, once or twice, this approach had succeeded, which is presumably why he still persisted with it...he had not yet realised, however, that this had only ever been the case *after* he had served lots of wine and *cognac*...his chances with either of the *Laverge* women were on the way from being "slim" to "nonexistent" already!)

"*Fous le camp, espèce de limace, je donnerai mon ordre à la serveuse*[21]" purred *Anne* in that elegant French, which, like her daughter's, was free of any regional accent.

---

21   "Fuck off, slug. I'll give my order to the waitress."

The waiter paused for an instant, then shrugged his shoulders, exhaled an expletive through lips pursed in archetypal French fashion, and moved on to the next table.

"*Maman*, you're becoming a feminist," observed *Marie*.

"What if I am? I've had reason enough..."

Discussion of this potentially fascinating subject was pre-empted by the arrival of the waitress, who had overheard *Anne's* diatribe. She took their orders, which turned out to be identical: *crudités* (raw carrots, cucumber, onions, sweet corn, peppers, and tomatoes in an olive oil, mustard, and vinegar dressing); fish soup with croutons and *rouille*[22]; *escargots* in parsley, garlic, and butter sauce; *entrecôtes de cheval*: their preferred *cuisson* being *à point* (medium rare)—the other options in France being *saignant* (bloody) or *bleu* (still neighing); *frites*; *salade mixte*; cheese; *île flottante avec crème fraîche*, then coffee with *calvados* (*pour "creuser un trou normand"* [23]).

The waitress also took their drinks order. *Marie* knew the arguments her mother and father had had about his consumption of *pastis*, so, much though she would have liked one herself as an *apéritif*, *Marie* acquiesced to her mother's choice of a *kir royal* instead. Both agreed, though, that a *pichet* of *blanc* to accompany the fish soup and *escargots*, and a *pichet* of *rouge* with the meat, were *exactement comme il faut*...

"*Maman*," said *Marie* mischievously, "did I see a bottle of *pastis* in the kitchen this morning?"

---

22   Not "rust" but a thick, red, garlic sauce.

23   "To dig a Norman hole"—a means of eating all day—a bit like the Roman feather down the throat without the vomiting. You down the *calvados* in one and it scours its way through the contents of your stomach...well, that's the theory...

"*Ma Chérie*," replied *Anne* with cool aplomb, "I still sometimes need to negotiate with an electrician or a plumber..."

"So, *Maman*, what is this little historical-research project?"

"*Oh...baf...ce n'est pas grande chose*...it's about an amusing, medieval English missionary called 'Skerne'... he went round the north of England with a 'Talisman' which was basically his means of seducing as many women as he could...he was a ridiculous fraud...yet it appears a twentieth-century cult has grown up around his name...*incroyable! Mais ce n'est pas important...ça m'amuse, tout simplement...*"

"How on earth did you discover such a topic?"

"A chance conversation with a gentleman I met in the library...he told me about Skerne...actually, I still see him there from time to time and I discuss my progress with him...he's very helpful...a *Monsieur Mochet...*"

"Does *Papa* know about this *Monsieur Mochet, Maman?*"

"Your *Papa* and I are divorced, remember, *Ma Petite*. We are both free to take other lovers if we wish...but this is certainly not the case here...we are merely... acquaintances with a common interest...*Monsieur Mochet* holds no sexual interest for me, I assure you..."

Her mother was a secondary school teacher of History—*une agrégée*—so her hours were not punishing... so it made sense...she had time for such "amusements" particularly so during the school holidays.

"And what about you, *Chérie*, how is your research going?"

"*Eh bien*, I'm still some way from curing all known diseases…"—*Marie* could be as arch as her mother—"but we are making some useful progress in my field of study…" She paused. "*Maman*, it's exciting…I love it…"

"*C'est bien!*" said the mother. "But still no *amant?*"

Chapter Thirteen

Marie sighed. Eventually, it always came to this. "*Non,* nor you, *non plus, Maman?*"

Anne was not to be out-manoeuvred. "*Non, Chérie,* but then I have had my fingers burned, *n'est-ce pas?* What is your excuse?"

"Why do I need an *excuse?* I enjoy my life, my job, my friends...if by chance a man came on the scene that I liked, then *voilà,* I'm free to go there...if I want..."

"But so far there has been no one with whom you would want to...go there?"

"*Non*...not in *Montpelier*...not so far..."

"But perhaps elsewhere?"

"No, not elsewhere either, *Maman*..." But *Marie* was remembering her meeting in this very restaurant with that huge American with the French surname and ridiculous *prénom...mais bien sûr,* she had remembered... *Beauchamp...Hatch Beauchamp*...he had had to spell his *prénom* for her...

They were both alone, at adjoining tables, and she had detected during his fluent conversation with the waiter a slight, unidentifiable, foreign accent. Intrigued, *she* had inaugurated the conversation, which was unusual—she was more used to cutting short conversations men started with her—and even more intrigued to discover he was American...very few Americans could speak her language as he did; most Americans didn't even know where France was! In a trice, it seemed, she was telling him about herself and her work and discovering what he did…so not only a francophone American but an Astrophysicist too, *Mon Dieu*! It was then she acknowledged that, actually, he was very attractive too…and obviously physically powerful, *Mon Dieu, Mon Dieu*! So she felt scarcely a smidgen[24] of shame when she complimented him on his French. This produced the greatest surprise of all: despite the expected aura of self-confidence, here was an American who could actually be modest and self-effacing!

"Thank you, I'm very pleased you think so," he had begun, "but learning a language with a good tutor… and I happen to have one of the best…a Frenchman no less…and having the opportunity to practice it and learn more *de temps en temps* on visits here…as I am now, *Mademoiselle*, thanks to you; this is not the same as absorbing it through exposure twenty-four hours a day from the day of your birth. There are so many things you incidentally pick up that way that I haven't—for instance I do not know the French names for a whole range of mammals…"

Marie could have had no idea that, as he said that, *Hatch* was wondering: "Yeah, what is the French fer a manatee, an okapi, a wolverine, an armadillo, a slender loris, a coypu, even a mole, fer Gawd's sake?"

"…Or parts of an automobile…" Similarly, "Yeah, what is the French fer a sparking plug, a head gasket, a timing belt, an overhead camshaft, a piston ring, even a dipstick, fer Christ's sake?"

---

24   The Author would be grateful to any reader who could arrange for him in order of magnitude: a tad, a smidgen, and an iota.

"…Or things to do with D.I.Y."

This time, *Marie* did notice that he appeared *un peu distrait*. What she could not have even guessed was that, at that moment, he was suddenly, inexplicably wondering, what if he married a French girl…this girl…and settled in France—and had to do some D.I.Y. "Lawdy," he was asking himself, "what is the French fer grout, skirting board, loft insulation, junction box, guttering, rawl plug, even screwdriver aw spanner, Gawd damn it?"

"I'm sorry, *Monsieur*, but I appear to have suddenly lost you," she had said teasingly.

She was astonished that he blushed and stammered for a few moments before regaining composure. He was charming…what a shame, she had thought, that the meeting was so fleeting…She had at that moment, which coincided with the arrival of his *moules frites*, looked at her watch and realised she had to leave…"*Bon appetit,*" she had said as she rose from her seat, but then could not resist a parting glance at him from the restaurant door…and he was looking straight back at her!

Mais aussi, chose incroyable! She believed she had seen him one evening a week later, staring up at her, as she crossed the bridge in *Chinon* on her way to her father's. *Une coïncidence ou une illusion?* She did not know!

"Where did you go to, my lovely?" Her mother interrupted her reverie.

"*Mon affaire, Maman. C'est méchant,* I'm well over twenty, you should not still want to look inside my head!"

"Or give a damn? I cannot stop loving you as a mother, simply because you are grown up, *Ma Petite*.

Forgive me, that's the reason I enquire…but I will stop. *Et de toute façon,* the first course is arriving…"

✳

Having dined well, *Anne* and *Marie* left the restaurant. As they were walking leisurely along the street, a squat man wearing a white, crumpled, three-piece, linen suit greeted them. *Marie* noticed a gold watch chain disappearing into a pocket of his waistcoat. The man's head was totally bald; he had flat, lobe-less ears, bulging eyes, almost amber in colour, and his chin merged into his neck with the merest ripple of a change of contour. His skin had a sallow, parchment-like quality, and the teeth he revealed as he smiled at both women were crooked and yellow. He reminded *Marie* of a repulsive, swollen toad…(*Marie* knew very well toads do not have ears or teeth…but the rest of him was toad-like…)

"*Madame Laverge,*" he said, taking *Anne's* hand to shake it. "*Quel plaisir…*and this must surely be your daughter…"

"*Marie,*" said her mother, "this is *Monsieur Mochet* who is helping me with my project."

"*Enchanté,*" said *Monsieur Mochet,* and he offered *Marie* his hand. She shook it, feeling at once that she had grasped cold, soft, moist worms. "*Marie…*yes, *Marie…*your mother has spoken to me of you…such a…delightful name…but I must not take up your time; this is yours together, *n'est-ce pas? Je vous laisse…à la prochaine… bonne continuation.*"

As they parted, *Marie* noticed the shadow he cast on the wall beside them. It must surely be an illusion caused by the irregularities of the stonework, she thought, but what she saw resembled for all the world a hideous, forkéd creature—like some gargoyle prized from the wall of a medieval church…

At seven in the evening, *Marie* announced that she was starving. *Anne* was happy to set about preparing the *souper* immediately. She began simmering the chicken noodle soup, while she chopped up the *lardons* and mushrooms and whisked the eggs for the omelette— *Marie* naturally helped, cutting up a whole *baguette*, preparing a dressing for the *salade verte*, and mixing mayonnaise into the bowl of potatoes that were already boiled, chopped, chilled, and sprinkled with chives. She pulled the cork out of a simple but fruity *vin de table*, and she and her mother sat down to the soup. Both found mopping it with bread preferable to spooning it—a habit they could unreservedly indulge in the privacy of their own home—and very quickly both soup and two thirds of the *baguette* were gone.

The omelette *Anne* quickly cooked was delicious; the salad, the potatoes, the conversation were equally so good, that in what seemed like next to no time, all—save possibly two slices of *baguette* and two half-glasses of wine to accompany the cheese—was gone. After the cheese *Anne* produced a little treat for her daughter—*une tarte aux pommes* accompanied by a sweet *muscat.* Then coffee and *cognac.*

Marie put the empty bottles with the others in the larder, then helped *Anne* wash up and tidy away, by which time it was close to eleven.

"*Maman*, that was a delicious meal," said *Marie*, rubbing her hand over her exquisitely flat stomach and abdomen. "I think I'm ready for bed."

"Me too."

Mother and daughter kissed.

"*Bonne nuits*" and "*dors biens*" were exchanged...then, just before they parted, *Marie* suddenly blurted: *Maman*, I hope you don't mind...but that *Monsieur Mochet*...I did not like him!"

Chapter Fourteen

Le quinze août began, as *Joachim Laverge* had predicted, and his daughter was grateful for the jumper, cardigan, scarf, and woollen skirt he had bought her, all of which, perforce, she now had to put on. The temperature had plummeted overnight from 32° Celsius to a glacial 21° C.

However, this was not going to impinge in any way yet on the *Duc* and his *entourage,* who were still in the Northeast of England where, of course, temperatures of 21° Celsius are considered tropical.

And besides, our narrative now returns to the evening of the 14th.

"*Seigneur,* will you be requiring my further services *ce soir?*" *Jean Le Taureau* respectfully asked the *Duc* at around half-nine that same evening.

The *Duc* had for his *chauffeur's* skills a deep respect and appreciation, and for the man himself a warm, but wholly chaste affection. But having divined the reason for this enquiry, he could not resist teasing him a little. With slow deliberation, the *Duc* frowned pensively, then tugged at the lobe of one of his perfectly proportioned, exquisitely depilated ears that followed the contours of his head with aerodynamic precision...and paused.

Then he smiled, revealing two rows of white, even teeth that even his American friend could envy.

"*Non, pas du tout...*the rest of the evening is yours, *Mon Brave.* Please make use of the Bentley if you wish..." and then the *Duc's* dark, intelligent eyes glinted with mischief: "and please tell Betty that we found her care of us this lunchtime as *impeccable* as she herself is *charmante...*"

Minutes later, *Jean Le Taureau* had reason himself to pause, at the pub's inner door, to eavesdrop on what a slim, young man of medium height was saying to Betty who was behind the bar.

"So you'll be finishing soon. It's a lovely, warm night! Fancy a little walk when you're done?"

"No thanks. I've already got a date, as it happens."

"Have you now? Well, you could always stand him up."

"I don't think so."

"Please yourself." At which the *petit morseau de merde* finished his drink and swayed towards the exit. As he passed *Jean Le Taureau,* he said quite audibly: "Snotty cow!"

At once, *Jean Le Taureau* was in the grip of a murderous rage, but since his first, impulsive killing he had learned circumspection. As was not the case with the two car vandals, this time there were witnesses to the scene in the bar, and a number of the locals knew of, or at least strongly suspected, his dalliance with Betty. And maybe because of this momentary reflection, another—and indeed rather amusing—idea suddenly struck him, perhaps nearly as appropriate an act of retribution for the man's rudeness and presumption as *Jean's* first impulse. *Jean* allowed thirty seconds or so to elapse, then followed his prey into the night. The man was wending his unsteady way across the green towards the The Wangthwaite Guest House. The burly ex-legionnaire moved with cat-like speed and stealth after him and intercepted him, just as he reached the gate to the house and had pulled the front door key from his pocket.

"Excuse me," said *Jean Le Taureau*, "you left something in the pub."

The man turned and looked with startled eyes at the person he had no idea had followed him. "What?"

"You left this in the pub." *Jean Le Taureau* made pretence of pulling something from his right-hand trouser pocket, and then swung all of his considerable weight into a right hook that landed flush on the jaw. The man fell forward—always the sign of a clean knockout—and lay inert on the grass verge beside the road.

Half a minute later, as *Jean* had felt sure he would be, the man was still unconscious when the Bentley purred to a stop beside him. After prizing the key from his hand, *Jean* had no difficulty lifting this slight individual into the car's cavernous boot.

Jean Le Taureau had already calculated distance, travel time, and the end of Betty's shift to a nicety. His journey took him past Throstlenest Hall—which was about five kilometres outside of the village—to a little, remote copse that was a kilometre further still.

The balmy, night air revived *Jean's* captive when his captor reopened the boot. The huddled, hapless heap was lifted bodily and deposited on the roadside. Gradually, the man took stock of his situation. His holiday had been a disaster from start to finish. Told that the North was a really friendly place, he been snubbed by every woman he'd approached, kneed in the groin in a bar, called a "southern puff" five times, asked who the fuck he was looking at seven times, and now this... He was resolved that if he survived this night, from now on he would venture no further north than Finchley!

"Wha...what are you going to do to me?" he stammered, looking at the looming *Languedocian* with mounting terror.

"Nothing, provided you do something for me!"

"What's that?"

"Give me your clothes."

"What!"

Jean Le Taureau cocked a ham-like, right fist and repeated his instruction. The man was already unbuckling his trouser belt.

When the man was completely naked, *Jean* folded the clothes with military neatness and placed them in the still-open boot of the Bentley. "You will find these in the garden of the guest house. Here is your key. In future, you will show Betty more respect, *n'est-ce pas?* Complain to the police, by all means. You will merely become a laughing stock! That is your way back." *Jean* lifted a hand and pointed. Then with a booming guffaw, he closed the car boot, got behind the wheel of the Bentley, and drove swiftly back to Wangthwaite.

The smell and feel of the leather seats in the back of the Bentley always heightened Betty's pleasure, but after a long stint in the pub, one *jouissance* often left her drowsy. So it was not until then that *Jean* told her of the wholly apt justice he had meted out to that annoying insect in the bar. *Jean* learned the man was a garden gnome salesman from Twickenham...so the *bestiole* was from the cradle of *La Patrie's* archrivals in rugby! *Jean's* course of action at once seemed all the more fitting... death would have been too good for the grub! Betty was instantly revived by *Jean's* account. The night was proceeding from very good to even better!

Meanwhile, the *Duc* had produced a decanter and three whisky tumblers that were clearly complementary to the other, magnificent, cut-glass, etched, ellipsoid vessels from which the three had drunk so splendid a selection of liquids. Now, the *Duc* was pouring them each *une bonne dose* of a rare, thirty-year-old Islay single malt—*Ceoinkinryroaig*[25]. He then produced a pipette from which he dispensed one drop of water into each glass..."To release the subtle *parfum* of the peat," he explained.

"*Eh bien, mes amis*, it is now time to tell you the rest of the matter. I learned from the Cardinal that just about every member of this grotesque sect of Skerne is known to the Vatican's...shall we say...intelligence. They are for the most part a ragbag collection of misguided

---

25   Pronounced "Sean Connery."

nonentities...hippies, dropouts, lesbians, frustrated career women with ideas above their station..." The *Duc* spat out this list with barely-concealed contempt. "So how on earth such a motley crew could have discovered the chest's hiding place, let alone masterminded its theft, was initially a mystery. However, a recent addition to their ranks may be the answer. He is someone of a different ilk altogether. His name is *Mochet...mais oui, un Français...*and he is someone shrouded in mystery. It appears he has independent means...he has no known employment, yet wherever he lives, he lives well. He has, over the past few years, changed location several times...but in each location have been disturbing rumours of...Devil worship! What his interest in the 'Talisman' might be, I do not know. I have learned from another source...the Cardinal is unaware of this...that all the printed material relating to Skerne and his Talisman—and indeed there is not much—has recently gone on loan to the public library of *Nevers*... commissioned by a local history teacher...who is *not* a member of the sect. Interestingly, however, *M. Mochet* is also presently located in *Nevers*...a coincidence? I think not. So, in two days time, that is where our 'adventure' will begin, *mes amis!* We will start, I think, by making the acquaintance of this history teacher—*Anne Laverge* is her name...

Anne Laverge—Nevers! This, also, was too much of a coincidence! At the prospect of perhaps seeing again that girl in the *chic cérise* suit—like a pretty flamingo— *Hatch* immediately wondered if someday he was going to make her his...if he only could, if she only would...

surely, it seemed destined to be…and then he wondered too: "What *is* the French fer 'flamingo', Goddam it?"

"One question, *Mon Cher Théodore*," interjected the maimed Russian, "vhy us?"

"As always, your questions do your intelligence credit, *mon ami*! The Cardinal, I am sure, has not told me all. However, the 'official' line is that the Vatican itself must *not* be seen by the sect to be actively seeking the chest's recovery, as it would compromise the present, shall we say, delicate negotiating position. Without the chest, whatever the sect of Skerne chose to say, they would be dismissed as a load of *fous*…with the chest, *alors, ça c'est autre chose*…and if it is not recovered, His Holiness still wants 'a hand to play.'

"We, however, are *inconnus*; our association with Our Holy Mother the Church is not public knowledge; we can proceed independently and covertly.

"However, I have my suspicions about *M. Mochet*…I believe he may be a foe against whom the Cardinal himself would not wish to be pitted, which is also why His Eminence has come to me…I have never before revealed this to you, *mes amis*, but in the ways of the Right-hand path, I am an *Ipsissimus*!"

"Ah what?" asked *Hatch*.

"An *Ipsissimus*!"

"Aw," murmured the American.

"Mm," added the Russian.

The *Duc* rose and laid a gentle, reassuring, but wholly chaste, hand on both his dear friends. "Let us now finish our whisky. In two days time, we leave for *La Belle France*…and by the way, let me caution you, tomorrow is the *quinze août.* The weather will change. Pack warm clothing. *Bonne nuit.*"

The *Duc* checked on *Tristan* and *Iseult*—both profoundly, contentedly dormant—then perhaps because of the stimulation of the conversation, or the effects of the *Ceoinkinryroaig,* he wasn't sure which, he decided to take a breath of fresh air. He opened the back door of his historic, monolithic, Anglo-Saxon domicile and strolled as far as the gates to the drive. He savoured the balmy air and turned back to the Hall when, suddenly...something fleeting had caught his eye...had his senses deceived him, had his *dose* of whisky been a little too *bonne,* or had he really seen a slightly-built, naked man scurrying furtively in the direction of the village?

Chapter Fifteen

The *Duc* had deliberated for some time before buying his first English car. *Bien sûr*, there were only two from which to choose, *à son avis*—a Rolls Royce or a Bentley. Famously, Rolls Royce would not reveal the power output of their vehicles…the firm simply said it was "adequate." The *Duc* saw in this understatement a reflection of the modesty he took pains to maintain in respect of his own superiority to other mortals in so many fields of human accomplishment. In the end, he had opted for the Bentley, partly because he found its timeless, classic beauty the more tastefully understated of the two, partly because the power output of the model he chose was said to be "more than adequate!"

He had then chosen the Jaguar as his second English car for its totally different styling. How well the car was named! It was wholly feline in appearance. And how refined yet eclectic was the urbane *Duc's* aesthetic sense! It was for this very reason a shark-nosed, futuristic *Citroën DS 23* nestled alongside a vintage *Bugatti* roadster in the capacious garage of *Le Château du Prat Ragé*.

It was in the Bentley that the determined trio made their intrepid way south. They were lodged simply but well in a roadside, rural inn close to Dover and took the eight o'clock ferry the following morning. Because of the sailing time, the slow procession through *la douane* and the hour's difference in time, it was late morning by the time they were *en route* in France.

They lunched for two hours in the delightful, medieval town of *Laon* perched on a hill on the borders of the *Champagne* region, and spent another two hours over dinner in the delightful, medieval centre of *Troyes*. The *Duc* had carefully chosen the itinerary so that it would be thus enhanced with historic interest, as well as culinary delight! How cerebral yet sensual were this cosmopolite's cultural proclivities!

Consequently, however, it was quite late when they reached *Nevers*.

In choosing their accommodation, the *Duc* had looked in the *Guide Michelin* and picked *L'Hôtel De La République*, which had been awarded five stars, no less. *Jean Le Taureau* had 'phoned ahead to learn, unfortunately—but unsurprisingly—that it was *complet*. The receptionist suggested trying *L'Hôtel Du Roi*, as it might have free rooms. So it proved. After consulting *Le Duc*, he had made the reservations. On entering the hotel, the reason for room availability was manifest. The owner was an obsessive Elvis fan. He had modelled the interior *décor* on that of "Graceland"…consequently, it was unspoilt by any good taste. However, it was very late…a decision whether to stay could not be delayed; it was now or never! The *Duc* had to surrender to practicality, but he was adamant…one night! "That's alright," he told the others, "but no more! That would be too much!"

His bedroom, the *Easy Come, Easy Go*, was across the corridor from *The Good Rocking Tonight* bridal suite, while further along the corridor, *Hatch Beauchamp, Alexandrov Slivovitch* and *Jean Le Taureau* were lodged respectively in rooms called the *King Creole*, the *Wild In The Country*, and the *Kid Galahad.*

The following morning, they fled from a menu offering mashed banana and peanut butter sandwiches to a nearby *café* for breakfast. With the arrival of a post-prandial *café* and a small glass of *eau de vie*, they began to plan their day. *Jean Le Taureau* was commissioned to find more suitable accommodation; *Hatch, Alexandrov Slivovitch*, and the *Duc* would find out where *Anne Laverge* lived; the *Duc* assigned himself the further task of contacting *Anne Laverge* as his alone.

Jean Le Taureau's mission was successfully achieved within half an hour—*L'Hôtel De La Paix*, only three *Michelin* stars, but wholly adequate, *à son avis.* He felt sure the *Duc* and his friends would not demur. He returned to *L'Hôtel du Roi* to settle their account and pack their cases into the boot of the car. As he entered the car park on his third and final trip, he saw an elderly, bow-leggéd woman dressed in a blue, floral overall, over a black dress allowing a ridiculously topiaried, miniature poodle to urinate on the nearside passenger door of the Bentley. At once, *Jean Le Taureau* was in the grip of a murderous rage, but the circumspection he had learned since his first, impulsive killing stood him in good stead. He waited. When she was back in the street and just out of sight—he had noted the direction she had taken—with the silent speed of a raptor that was so surprising in one so big, he put the last case in the car, and then began the pursuit of his prey. Within a minute, he could not believe his luck. She was tying the laughable animal's leash to a lamppost before she mounted the steps into a *pharmacie*. The dog was untied within seconds, and it and *Jean Le Taureau* had gone "walkies" round the nearest corner. Two blocks further along the street on which he found himself, he came across a dark alley in which were placed two municipal wheelie-bins. He pulled the dog into the alley. A quick twist of the neck dispatched the ludicrous mutt. He placed its corpse beneath two large bin bags in one of the bins. There had been no witnesses. He had worn his *chauffeur's* gloves throughout. *Fait accompli!*

As he retraced his steps, he lit a celebratory *Gauloise*. Outside the *pharmacie*, a white-coated young woman was trying to console the hysterical old hag. It was all he could do to prevent a triumphal guffaw from erupting from his mouth.

He drove the Bentley to their new accommodation and installed the cases in their respective rooms. Later, he would have to make arrangements to wash the car. For the moment, his time was his own. He went to a nearby bar and ordered a quadruple *pastis* to accompany his second, celebratory *Gauloise.*

The *Duc, Hatch,* and *Alexandrov Slivovitch*, meanwhile, were enjoying another *café* and *eau de vie* in another bar. They had acquired a town plan and a telephone directory. Unfortunately for them, names in French telephone directories are grouped by village and district, and as this was the very information they wished to discover—in which village or district *did Anne Laverge live?*—their task would be painstaking.

By lunchtime, they had listed all the *Laverges* in the directory, and eliminated those with the wrong initials, which left them with a list of nine. The break for lunch was very welcome. *Hatch* suggested they go to the restaurant he had dined in last year. He couldn't remember its name, but he knew how to get there.

"*Mais c'est bizarre!*" exclaimed the *Duc* when the three of them were looking at the restaurant from the opposite side of the street.

"How is zat, *mon ami?*" asked the crippled Ex-Soviet.

"*Mais, regarde! Le nom!*"

Alexandrov Slivovitch looked at the name of the establishment and, at once, all was clear! "*Le Cul de Blaireau.*" He uttered an unspeakable Russian oath, then said, "Our...how you zay...our local brew! *Mais, Mon Cher Théodore,* zis is auspicious, *n'est-ce pas?* It is a good sign!"

"Let us hope so!"

"And let's go eat," added *Hatch.*

The trio entered the restaurant. At once, both the *Duc* and *Alexandrov Slivovitch* sensed a change in the huge American's composure. They looked at their friend and saw that he was immobile, wide-eyed, and starting to redden. The *Duc* followed the direction of his gaze to a table at which were seated two beautiful women, possibly sisters, possibly mother and daughter... the elder of the two had a suspicion of grey in her short, black hair; the younger a cascade of black hair falling over her shapely shoulders. They seemed engrossed in conversation...then the younger woman looked in their direction...

༺❧༻

Anne Laverge was listening intently to her daughter and was utterly surprised when *Marie* abruptly stopped speaking mid-sentence. *Anne* looked at her daughter who was looking elsewhere with wide eyes. She followed the direction of her daughter's gaze to three men standing just inside the restaurant. One was young, huge, and ruggedly attractive; the second, young, slight in build, facially scarred, wearing an eye-patch and leaning on an elegant cane. The third, older than the other two, was, nonetheless, the one she found the most interesting; he was tall, lean, and aristocratic, with dark, intelligent eyes, an aquiline nose, a noble, perfectly-proportioned mouth, and ears sculpted aerodynamically to his head— altogether a handsome, charismatic man. She looked back at her daughter.

"*Mais, alors, Ma Chérie,* you are blushing!" she exclaimed with surprise.

Chapter Sixteen

Alexandrov Slivovitch's French was equally as fluent as *Hatch's*, though perhaps a tad (or should that be a smidgeon, or an iota?) more heavily accented. True, *he* didn't know either the French for yak, musk ox, potto, platypus, echidna, or wombat; flywheel, constant-velocity joint, crankshaft, tappet, anti-roll bar, damper, or wheel trim; wainscoting, beading, dowel, sander, wood filler, drill, drill bit, Allen key, plane, cement mixer, plasterer's float, pointing trowel, wallpaper scraper, wallpaper paste, roller, chisel, extension lead, tile cutter, or spirit level. But presently, this was of no concern to him. (Had it been, he may well have reflected that, judging by the construction of their garden walls, the French do not know the French for spirit level either!)

It was he who had apprised the situation the most quickly, saw the re-establishment of composure in both his friend and the girl, and so said audibly enough for all parties to hear...

(Which, of course, he knew, was the point of speaking audibly. Once, though, in Moscow, at the start of a lecture he had delivered on the hunting tactics of narwhal pods—a subject in which he was expert partly through bitter experience—he had most audibly asked the customary question: "Can you hear me at the back?" and someone had said "No." Only after brutal interrogation by the KGB was it learned that this person was not a trouble-making dissident but a deaf, long-sighted lip-reader!)

...Anyway, audibly, *Alexandrov Slivovitch* said, "*Mon ami*, I think here is an acquaintance of yours ... please do me the honour of introducing me to such charming company," and was heard by all concerned. He could not have been aware, however, how welcome every other member of his audience found his proposition.

Hatch, who had indeed regained self-possession, took the initiative. "So nice to see you again. May I introduce my friends, *Marie?*"

He would have been enraptured had he known the flutter her heart gave at the realisation he had remembered her name!

"*Mais bien sûr, Monsieur*," interjected her mother before *Marie* had re-regained her self-possession. "You are obviously already acquainted with my daughter! It would be a great pleasure to make your acquaintance, too, and that of your friends!" She looked at the three men, her eyes lingering on the *Duc*. "Are you here *pour manger, messieurs?* We have only just arrived ourselves. Perhaps you might like to join us?"

The introductions made, the trio seated themselves opposite the two delectable *Françaises* and, immediately, a waitress came to the table with menus and asked them for their order of *apéritifs*. *Hatch* was dimly aware for an instant of a young waiter skulking in the background, louring in their direction with a look of sullen defeat. *Hatch* paid no heed, however; he and *Marie* were already becoming engrossed in conversation.

They all began to discuss what to eat. Meanwhile, *Anne* could not help but admire the well-manicured fingers attached elegantly to the slender, aristocratic hands with which the *Duc* was holding his menu, nor could she help approving either the deep, resonant baritone—which she had initially only briefly detected—when the *Duc* flatteringly asked her what she would recommend.

One could have forgiven *Alexandrov Slivovitch* for not being without rancour at the injuries he had sustained, and particularly as they meant he no longer received the same interest his two friends received—as indeed he *once* had—from members of the opposite sex. In a situation like this, a lesser mortal might have begun to harbour dark thoughts, to have perhaps pondered in which woman's glass to pour his toxin, were it only ready, so that either the *Duc* or *Hatch* might know at first hand what it was like to be deprived of such company, or to twist and press the knob of his cane so that a spray of hydrofluoric acid might give one or other of these two exquisite women the bitterness of knowing what it was to be disfigured and an amputee. Perhaps, indeed, such feelings lay suppressed in his subconscious. But *Alexandrov Slivovitch* was aware at that moment only of finer feelings; his friends' pleasure was his!

But it would turn out that his partial detachment from the interactions that were developing, would give him an insight that, in the fullness of time, would be crucial! For he learned by overhearing parts of *both* conversations that the *Laverge* family were *Anne, Joachim,* and *Marie*…and all these names had a disturbing, elusive resonance for him that it would take him some time to identify...

"So, *messieurs*," asked *Anne*, "what brings you to *Nevers*?"

"Please, let me answer your question, *Madame*," said the *Duc*, "if you will permit me, by first asking *you* one? Are you the same *Anne Laverge* who is currently researching the subject of 'The Talisman of Skerne?'"

Anne's dark, liquid, almond eyes, in which the *Duc* was already teetering on the brink of wallowing, if indeed not quite *yet* drowning, opened wide, becoming enormous pools of amazement.

"*Mais alors! Mais oui!* But how could you know this?"

"*A toute à l'heure*, if you will again permit me, please, *Madame* to answer your original question, we have come to *Nevers* to find *you!*"

Before she could make any response, *Alexandrov Slivovitch* turned an ironic, but in no way rancorous, eye on his huge, American friend. "*Mais, mon ami*, you haf been a little coy, *n'est-ce pas?* Not revealing zat you already knew *la famille Laverge* in *Nevers?* Hafing us spend a whole morning trawling through ze telephone directory, vhen you simply needed to bring us here!"

Discountenanced and reddening, again, *Hatch* inadvertently reverted for a moment to his native tongue. "Aw shoot, *Alexandrov!* Thar was naw way a' knawing these were the same fawlks, Goddam it! Aind besides, *Marie* hadn't given me her address or phawn number... Aind thar was naw way a'knawing tha'd be here!"

Marie had not understood a word of what *Hatch* had said, other than her own name, but nonetheless had decided at once that he sounded altogether more sexy when he spoke French!

Regaining composure, *Hatch* apologised for this lapse of *politesse* and reverted to French, which *Marie* immediately found more sexy. "I thought it was probably a coincidence," he said.

"I don't believe in coincidences," said *Anne* and the *Duc* at the same time. The wry smiles the two then instantly exchanged gave each the opportunity to admire the other's display of decidedly dazzling dentition. But between them both had occurred another, subtler, understanding, which left the *Duc* on the horns of a dilemma! He had rehearsed prior to this meeting a fiction to explain it, which walked a *very* fine line between truth and downright deception. But his logic had already told him that this—as he'd now discovered—*superbe* woman was probably *not* party to the machinations of the sect of Skerne, and his intuition now wholly confirmed this. So he made the decision there and then that he would take her into his confidence to an extent he had not previously intended. But she was nevertheless on the periphery of something potentially evil, so, for her sake, he still had to be cautious.

"Now, to answer your second question, *Madame*. We, too, are interested in the Talisman, but perhaps for reasons, which I will tell you shortly, are other than your own. But it was not difficult to discover that all the printed material relating to this 'artefact' had been recently commissioned by the town's library at *your* request. That someone else associated with the Talisman was also living in the same town seemed like too much of that thing neither of us, as we have just discovered, believe in... *une coïncidence!*"

"Who is this person?"

"Someone as yet we have never met, a *Monsieur Mochet.*"

"But I know him! *M. Mochet* pointed me in the direction of the subject!"

"I see." The *Duc* did not disclose that *Mochet* almost certainly knew far more about the subject than did *Anne Laverge*, so why had he encouraged her to research it? He was puzzled.

"Did you know that just over a week ago, the Talisman and its chest were stolen?"

"*Mais non!*" Her dark, liquid, astonished, almond eyes opened to their widest compass—their depths never more invitingly profound—at this revelation. "But how? Its location is a secret closely guarded by The Church! Nowhere is this place ever named!"

"Yet, somehow, it has been discovered; the Talisman is gone! And the thieves are putting their trophy to mischievous use. We are acting, shall we say, as covert agents of The Church to recover it. *Madame*, I have just taken you into my confidence and I beg you, count on you, not to betray it! But you asked the question, and even after so brief an acquaintance, I decided you were a person that deserved no dissimulation."

In contrast to *Marie* and *Hatch's* erubescence, *Anne's* was a merest hint of the most delicate rose, yet blush nonetheless she did. And the *Duc*, with that refined sensibility that so distinguished the man was both pleased and sorry at the same time to have been its cause!

"But the *hors d'oeuvres* arrive! Let us eat!" He thus averted any further embarrassment with his usual aplomb!

And they ate splendidly! At the end of the meal, the *Duc* had his way and paid. *Anne* insisted she feed them all *chez elle* the following evening. But *Hatch* and *Marie*, it transpired, had already arranged to eat out together; and *Alexandrov Slivovitch* made his apologies, as he had promised *Jean Le Taureau*, their *chauffeur*, another chess lesson then. So it was agreed the three pairs would dine in three locations.

They left the restaurant. As they did so, *Marie* had a fleeting glimpse of a figure rounding the nearest corner. She had not recognised who it was, but was disconcerted to see for a few moments longer the person's shadow on the nearby wall, the same shadow she had seen outside here previously…like a hornéd demon!

"*Maman!*" she cried. "I think that was *M. Mochet*! Is he stalking us?"

In an instant, *Hatch* bounded in pursuit only to find himself looking at a bewilderment of people in the street into which he turned. Which one might be *Mochet*? He had no idea! So he returned to the group.

Shortly afterwards, they said their *au revoirs*.

Jean Le Taureau had left a message for his employer and his friends with the *patron* of the café where the trio had agreed to rendezvous. The man knew them immediately and passed on the name and location of *L'Hôtel de La Paix*, which, indeed, was just a stroll away.

The Talisman of Skerne   by Tom Carr

"... *Mochet*! Is he stalking us?"

Two more quadruple *pastis,* plus the wine with his lunch, and an obligatory *calvados* after it, had strongly suggested to *Jean* that *une sieste* would be a good idea, particularly if his services as *chauffeur* were to be required that evening...but he had first taken the car to a carwash, nonetheless, reasoning—he thought, reasonably—that, anyway, his size must mean that alcohol was far more diluted per cubic centimetre in him than the same quantity would be in, say, a micro-cephalic dwarf!

As it turned out, his employer and his friends had no intention of straying farther than the *hôtel* restaurant that evening, so *Jean* returned to his bar for more *pastis.*

The *Duc, Hatch,* and *Alexandrov Slivovitch* had a light *souper* of *cuisses de grenouille* and *crevettes à l'ail* that evening, lubricated with *Chablis.* A *Beaujolais* enhanced the delights of the cheese. Then *café* and a *digestif.*

Perhaps it was the *calvados* that unlocked that elusive memory.

"*Шум!*" exclaimed *Alexandrov Slivovitch,* suddenly, to the startlement of his friends. "But how could I haf not seen zis straight avay! Tell me, vhich other family had a mother and father called Anna and Joachim and a daughter called Mary, mm?"

"Lawdy, lawdy," gasped *Hatch.* "The Holy Family!"

"*Nom d'un nom!*" exhaled the *Duc.* "*Mais oui,* now that you have pointed it out, *c'est evident!* Why didn't *I* see it? You have had a moment of genius, *mon ami!*"

"But vhat does it mean?"

"I don't know, *Mon Brave*...let us still take our time. Tomorrow, I may learn much more about *M. Mochet* in the delightful company of *Anne Laverge* than perhaps we would ever have done through tedious hours leafing again through a telephone directory...

"And, *Hatch*, you may learn things too...By the way, where did you say *Marie's* father now lives?"

"*Chinon.*"

"*Vraiment! Incroyable!* Until very recently, *M. Mochet* also lived in *Chinon!*"

There and then, the *Duc* made a decision. "*Mes amis*, the day after tomorrow, we will visit *Joachim Laverge*. I do not want to involve his daughter or ex-wife too much in our investigations, and besides, though we could ask *Marie*, perhaps, to ask *him* some questions she would not necessarily know where to go next with his answers..."

"*Шум!*" exclaimed *Alexandrov Slivovitch*, suddenly, again to the startlement of his friends.

"*Laverge! Laverge! Mon Cher Théodore*, could this be perhaps a corruption of *La Vièrge? Marie La Vièrge?* Mary The Virgin?"

The *Duc* looked again with admiration at his handicapped comrade. "*Et en plus*, the corruption itself, if indeed it *is* such, has another meaning, are you not aware? *Une verge*[26] is a birch or a cane, but it is also *argot* for...what are those ludicrous, gross Anglo-Saxon

---

26   Seeing the sign "Soft verges" often brings a smile to the English-speaking, visiting French person's face. Continuing loosely in this vein, it is likely computer nerds are impressing girls these days by vaunting what their "dongles" can do far more than they ever did in the days when all they had to vaunt were their "3½ inch floppies."

terms…a todger, a prick, a John Thomas, a knob, a cock, a willy!

(How much wider was the *Duc's* English vocabulary, both friends had simultaneously, yet independently, reflected, than was their French!)

"And what has brought us here?" continued the *Duc* with superb rhetoric. "*Mais oui!* The search for the golden todger, the golden prick, the golden John Thomas, the golden knob, the golden cock, the golden willy…*La Verge d'Or!*

"*Non, vraiment,* this time I am totally in earnest, I do not believe in coincidences! Not in this instance! Not at all!"

Chapter Seventeen

Jean Le Taureau was again in the grip of a murderous rage. Unfortunately[27], this time, there was no victim to hand...

True, *Jean* was an iota (or should that be a tad or a smidgeon?) hungover, but principally, while valeting the interior of the Bentley, he had again encountered The Mystery Of The White Flecks...No matter how often he vacuumed the car's black, luxurious, deep-pile carpet, within forty-eight hours, mysteriously, white flecks reappeared on it! What were they? Where did they come from?

They were not cigarette ash! Perhaps decades ahead of his time, the *Duc* insisted that those who smoked should not do so, either in his houses or his cars. This affected mainly only *Jean Le Taureau* and *Alexandrov Slivovitch*, who had an addiction to, respectively, *Gauloises* and *Sobranie* Cocktail. (Actually the good *Duc* himself was not averse to occasionally savouring a fine *Roberto Fonseca* Cuban cigar; though nonetheless observing the same locational restrictions he demanded of others—for such was the man's innate, sublime sense of fairness!)

Jean paused in his work, stood erect and bellowed entirely for his own satisfaction at the infuriating phenomena: "You Bastards! You Bastards!"

---

27   Of course that should have been "fortunately"...

However, assuming the fulmination of this large, enraged person was directed at *them*, two slightly built, middle-aged, passing joggers broke into an adrenaline-fuelled, lung-bursting sprint away from his immediate vicinity. Unfortunately, consequently, within minutes, one of them suffered a fatal, cardiac infarction.

It would have mollified *Jean Le Taureau* somewhat had only he known!

Early that evening, however, the *Duc's chauffeur* was in wholly different fettle, his *blood-pastis* imbalance having been rectified. So he drove the white-fleck-free Bentley with matchless precision and parked outside the *appartement* of *Anne Laverge*.

Jean waited beside the sumptuous limousine, until the *delectables Laverges,* who had both come down, had met the *Duc* and Hatch at the street door.

"*Seigneur,*" the faithful *chauffeur* then asked, "when should I collect you?" The title of *Seigneur,* even more so than the sight of the Bentley, had caused the luscious, dark eyes of both women to grow wide with amazement.

"But, *Mon Brave,* you have your chess evening," replied the *Duc.* "Enjoy it…and if I know *Alexandrov Slivovitch*…also your vodka! The town, I am sure, has a fine taxi service. *A bientôt.*"

So he had no need to be there when the *Duc* came out! He was first amazed and then grateful. His amazement and gratitude were not long after tempered, however, by the reflection that maybe the good *Duc* was trying to make a good impression! (One cannot spend one's *service militaire* in the French Foreign Legion without emerging *un peu cynique, n'est-ce pas?*)

As *Jean Le Taureau* got back into the Bentley, *Hatch* was responding to the reaction of the two women. "*Théo* does not like to publicise the fact, but he is, actually, *Théodore Le Duc de Cornsai-Tantobé!*"

Anne was immediately impressed by her dinner guest's modesty. But then reflected—perhaps a little cynically too, although *she* had never been in the French Foreign Legion—that perhaps her dinner guest was trying to impress her with his modesty. But then she was again impressed that—if so—*she* was someone who in his estimation was worth impressing!

Anne observed the *Duc's* reaction. He raised resigned eyebrows, shrugged his shoulders and extended his arms at the end of which were slender, outstretched hands with aristocratic palms, attached to the ends of which were long, elegant fingers with exquisitely manicured nails. "*Ce n'est pas grande chose!* Today we live in *une République…*these days the former Nobility are Noble in name only, unless one is noble in essence, and one does not need a title to be *that…*"

Mm! Now that *was* impressive!

"Please come in, *Seigneur Le Duc*," *Anne* purred with—to the *Duc*—delightful and wholly seductive humour. "I do hope my *terrine de lièvre* is to your taste." And it was now the *Duc* who was impressed!

For both couples the evening became a turning point in their lives.

Anne and the *Duc* found something more than the succulence of the jugged hare to savour. Both discovered a deep rapport that led to their poignant, pivotal moment.

For the first time ever, the *Duc* spoke openly to another human being about the sole, but most profoundly sad, event of his life. The safari to the Okavanga Delta, those incautious, fateful, few moments while his attention was elsewhere, the enraged, foraging hippopotamus, and the loss of his young wife and the son and heir she was bearing... *Mais oui*, since then, he had taken other women to his bed[28]... *après tout*, he was French...but he had never taken another into his heart! But, finally, to speak to someone of his tragedy was carthartic...and when he suddenly realised he could safely bare the innermost secrets of his soul to this wonderful woman ...it was as if in that long-barren part of the garden of his being, another exotic bloom had miraculously taken root and the bright, elusive butterfly of love would have intoxicating nectar again on which to gorge, an iridescence with which to be enthralled!

For the first time since the realisation that the childhood sweetheart she had once adored enough to marry was an obsessive-compulsive, emotionally-stunted, unhygienic, drunken, flatulent wuss, had *Anne* ever allowed herself to believe any man could be anything other than a temporary amusement. But, finally, to discover an attractive, urbane, witty, intelligent man

28   Though he had always gone to confession afterwards...and said two decades of the Rosary for his penance!

who also was as interested in what she had to say as in what he had to tell her... *alors!* Perhaps, finally, here was someone for whom she might become a climbing rose and grow and intermesh into the trellis of his life!

For *Marie* and *Hatch* their evening had started with small talk and a little shyness. *Their* pivotal moment began when *Hatch* had been bold enough to admit how much she had stayed in his mind since their first meeting. And how this act of boldness had been rewarded! For she had rushed to tell him that his experience had been the twin of her own!

And then, they had settled more and more into an ease with each other that neither would have believed they would ever discover. At times, *Hatch* had even felt a little overawed by the obvious affection this quick-witted, sensitive, multifaceted, wholly-glorious girl was showing *him*...that indeed he was mere, plain chowder to her rich, seasoned gumbo...

What was so refreshing for *Marie* was the company of a man who was not self-obsessed like the intense *précieux* she seemed to encounter in abundance in the *milieu* in which she worked. Perhaps it was because *Hatch* had never seen, much less ever been in thrall to the cinematic *oeuvre* of *Jean-Luc Cliché* in which couples agonised *ad nauseam* over the significance of every nuance of feeling...

This ruggedly attractive, *powerful* man was such a delightful mixture of confidence and shyness, of erudition and innocence…and he showed so guilelessly and unaffectedly, so spontaneously and honestly his appreciation of *her…comment c'était formidable!*

Had *Marie* finally found a man with whom a relationship would be like the synchronous, symbiotic complementarity of wholly disparate, yet mutually dependent, organs in a body? Could *she* perhaps be the pancreas to *his* duodenum?

When *Marie* and *Hatch* arrived at the street door to her mother's apartment, *Marie* consciously moved onto the step to minimise their height difference. But she would receive only his smile! *Hatch* was so very much the southern gent, he would never presume to expect a kiss at the end of a first date! *Marie* was as touched as she was disappointed.

She could not have known (but no more would she have wished to…children cannot bear to even think about what their parents might be up to *in that way!*) that at that very moment, on the other side of the door, the *Duc* with gallic gallantry was raising her mother's hand and brushing the back of it with a labial touch of the most exquisite, sensual subtlety that began to melt her mother wholly…

For *Anne* and the *Duc* and *Marie* and *Hatch*, then, the evening had been superb. Little could they have guessed how differently things would appear within a mere twenty-four hours!

Chapter Eighteen

At just before eight the next morning, the *Duc, Hatch,* and *Alexandrov Slivovitch* settled into the sumptuous, leather, rear seats of the still-white-fleck-free Bentley, putting themselves in the capable, gloved hands of the loyal ex-legionnaire, who harnessed all of the car's more-than-adequate power to whisk them effortlessly towards *Chinon* and their afternoon rendezvous with *Joachim Laverge.*

They dined simply yet well at a roadside, rural *auberge* and, at twenty-eight minutes past two to the second, having left the delightful, historic centre of *Chinon,* were crossing the bridge over *La Loire. Marie's directions* were *impeccables.* It was exactly another two minutes to her father's home. They arrived there at precisely the time they had arranged!

Joachim Laverge lived in a detached, two-storey house of recent construction, which was surrounded by high, bare breezeblock walls, built without the use of a spirit level. Standing nearly half a metre taller than and behind the walls were rows of flowering shrubs.

The three men entered the garden. At once they forgot the decrepitude of the surrounds, as they marvelled at the pulchritude of the grounds! These were an exemplar of proportion, colour and shape, a paradigm of judgement, skill, and vision, an epitome of the tilth and husbandry of a horticulturist *sans pareil*!

It was obvious at once to the *Duc,* that whatever the man's weaknesses (and *Anne* had listed several), nonetheless, *Joachim Laverge,* too, had contributed richly to the clearly superb genome expressed in the daughter—and now that his equally genetically superior friend (*Hatch's* physical splendour and incisive intellect proclaimed it) seemed so wisely on the brink of selecting such a mate with whom to breed, why, this gave the sage, beneficent, urbane, learned aristocrat a joy that welled to overflowing in his noble breast!

"*Monsieur De Cornsai-Tantobe?*" asked a quiet, slightly quavering voice.

The *Duc* and his two friends turned from the splendour of the garden to the source of the question. A slightly-built man of more than medium height was emerging from the doorway of the house. The *Duc* noticed at once the slight oedema of the skin of his face, the slight reddening of his nose and cheeks, the slight tremble in his right hand, the slight tic in his left eye, the slight totter in his gait and, as he drew close, the slight miasma of aniseed that enveloped him... and recalled *Anne's* dismay at the man's distressing problem—although the loss of *Anne Laverge,* thought the *Duc* in commendably impartial mental mitigation, would surely prompt any man to plunge into the oblivion of *pastis, n'est-ce pas!* But which had it been? The cause, the result, or the *pretext* of that loss...or perhaps all of these things...or yet even more strangely, possibly *none of them?*

The confident, sophisticated, subtle appraiser of situations that was, *par excellence,* the *Duc de Cornsai-*

Tantobé immediately took stock and the initiative[29]. "Indeed, *Monsieur, enchanté.* Please let me introduce my two friends...this is *Hatch Beauchamp* and this is *Alexandrov Slivovitch Romanov...*" adding at the raising of *Joachim Laverge's* slightly twitching eyebrows: "*Oui,* indeed a member of that royal and tragic lineage, but if you will permit, *Monsieur,* we prefer now to draw a veil over that despicable episode of history. Please let me compliment you on your exquisite garden! *C'est magnifique!*

"*Mais...Toc!* It's simply what I do for a living!" he said with a Gallic pout and shrug. "I plan, construct, and maintain gardens, both for *clients privés* and for the municipality." But *Joachim Laverge* was clearly pleased! "I am pleased" (he admitted in subtle subterfuge) "to say that *Chinon* last year won a national award for its flowers—I am proud to have had some great part in that...However," (and finally the admission was frank) "thank you for your compliments...

"My garden is my showroom...*Bien, alors,* how can I be of service? *Mais pardon.* Can I offer you something while we talk...I have just opened a bottle of *pastis*...or there is wine...or cognac?"

"Un *pastis* would be wholly acceptable, *merci,*" intoned the *Duc* in that deep, resonant baritone that had recently so impressed this man's ex-wife. "But a moment, if we may. *Kemo Sabe* and *Hutini!* My favourite cacti, *Monsieur!* And is that exotic orchid over there a *Bilhipypa?* How extraordinary! Our tastes coincide again.

---

29   I am sure the discerning Reader will have spotted a spot of zeugma!

Mais chose absolument incroyable! How can you grow such a magnificent *Climbing Ahura* in this northerly clime?"

As his ex-wife had been the day before, *Joachim Laverge* was impressed by this man—though it should be said neither to the same extent nor certainly in anything like the same way!

"*Monsieur*," exclaimed the gratified gardener. "I'm impressed with both your knowledge and your taste. It is true, the *Climbing Ahura* needs a lot of care...Yet *I* have a special *penchant* for the succulents...their shapes are so varied and interesting, *n'est-ce pas?* Nature's surreal sculptures! But I have a great affection for my old stalwarts too!"

Joachim Laverge pointed to the tall shrubs covered in flowers of various hues, growing against the inside of all of the garden's undulating walls. "They give me privacy *and* beauty! *Laurel.* And hardy! *Mais oui!* Once they are established they require virtually no maintenance!"

"*Mais, venez.* I will pour drinks and then we can discuss...how I might be of assistance."

They followed *Joachim Laverge* into his kitchen-diner. Taking up easily half of the surface area of the room was a large, antique pine table. On it was a half-empty[30] bottle of *pastis,* a carafe containing a modicum of water, and a glass whose dregs told clearly their creamy, cloudy, incriminating tale!

Joachim Laverge brought three more glasses to the table, recharged the carafe with Evian water and added to it several ice-cubes that he had bludgeoned violently from their tray. The drinks were poured. The *Duc*

30   Given the rather pitiable state of *Joachim Laverge* it would have been inappropriate to say "half-full."

considered the dose of *pastis* given to him and his two friends a redoubtable double; that which *Joachim* poured himself easily a sizable sextuple! Mais *quand même!*[31]

The *Duc* wasted no more time. "*Monsieur*, I will not dissemble. I am willing to pay for your time...indeed I insist, you must please tell me your usual consultancy fee...but I confess we are not here to enlist your services...simply to ask you some questions.

"May I come directly to the point? Have you ever had any dealings with a...*Monsieur Mochet?*"

The whole of *Joachim Laverge's* face twitched slightly.

"*Mais oui!* Do you know this detestable toad?"

"*Non!* We do not know him...we only know *of* him. Why do you describe him as 'detestable?'"

"Because, unlike you, *Monsieur*, he dissembled! He came here and talked to me about what he would like me to do to the grounds of his house...he showed me the grounds of his house...a substantial property out of town...requiring much work...but with so much potential...I drew up plans and we discussed them and modified them...indeed we became for a while quite friendly...then I sent him an interim bill, and nothing! I rang him about this. The 'phone was no longer connected. I went to his house...it was empty. Indeed, it was not even his. He had rented it! If only I had had the opportunity to catch up with him just once before he left...I would have wiped the floor with him...slightly!"

Joachim Laverge swallowed a good *bouchée* of *pastis*.

The keenly intelligent *Duc* reflected for a moment.

---

31   All the same; whatever.

"*Alors!* You say you became friendly. In what way, if I may ask? *Par example*, what did you discuss?"

"Mmm...the garden project, mainly...I believe we may have shared some personal details...about our families, our past...you know, how these things can arise... But excuse me, *Monsieur*, why do you want to know this?"

"*Monsieur*, I will answer *your* question if you will permit *me* to ask you one more, first. Did he ever talk to you about...The Talisman of Skerne?"

"*Quoi? Non. Absolument pas!*"

"Without boring you with the detail, *Monsieur*, the Talisman of Skerne is a...Christian relic that has gone missing...and we have been commissioned by Our Holy Mother The Church to track it down and recover it...and *Monsieur Mochet* may well be implicated in its disappearance...indeed, it may intrigue you to know he is currently in *Nevers* and, in fact, has persuaded your ex-wife to take something of an interest in this relic too..."

"He seems to take something of an interest in my family..."

"That's as it may be!" murmured the *Duc* somewhat dismissively. "But this Talisman entered in no way into your conversations with him, *Monsieur*? Ever? You are certain of this?"

"*Absolument.* I'd never heard of the thing till you mentioned it!"

"How bizarre!" The *Duc* was pensive, then muttered more to himself than any around him..."But I do not believe in coincidence of this sort...what is going on?"

Then directly to *Joachim Laverge*: "Why did he waste your time, I wonder?"

Both men looked at each other, pouting lips, raising eyebrows, and shrugging shoulders—that quintessential yet strangely charming, French way of showing bewilderment!

∽✌∽

The burly, gloved, loyal ex-Legionnaire harnessed again all of the Bentley's more-than-adequate power and began whisking the good *Duc* and his two friends effortlessly on their way.

Perhaps nine minutes, fifty-nine and ninety-nine hundredths of a second had passed, roughly, before anyone spoke.

It was *Alexandrov Slivovitch* who then did: "*Mon Cher Théodore*, I vill grant zat ve haf passed a not altogether unpleasant day...but haf ve learned anything?"

The good *Duc* acknowledged the question was a fair one...yet could not accept their time had been entirely wasted. Something *had* been learned—he knew it—but he could not yet see what it was! It bothered him.

Sometime later to the nanosecond, the *Duc* suddenly said again, "Turn off into the next town, *Jean, s'il te plait*. I need time to think and perhaps a drink will...how can I put this... *me débloquer un peu*! Something bothers me..."

So, as it chanced, they would look back in *Angers*[32] at what they already knew and hopefully the *Duc* would fathom what else today might have told them.

---

32   This was a particular relief for *Jean Le Taureau*, who had been wondering for a while now how to tell the others he was driving in the wrong direction.

The two friends watched with grave anticipation as the *Duc* sipped his first *cognac*, calming their nerves with their own.

Suddenly, the *Duc* was deblocked! He laughed sardonically (and did so wholly appropriately) before exclaiming, "*Joachim* himself told us plainly what we wanted to know! How could I have missed it at the time! How did he put it? He was referring to *Mochet*. 'He seems to take something of an interest in my family'…"

"*Voilà!*" continued the *Duc*. "*Mochet* has been courting…or how did *Marie* put it? Stalking! *Mais oui, elle avait raison! Monsieur Mochet* has been stalking *Les Laverges* primarily because of *them*! *Mon cher ami*! You may have provided the key! Joachim, Anna and Mary! This has to be significant! But to know how, we *definitely* need to recover The Talisman! I am certain it holds the answer! *Allons-y!*"

With the capable, gloved hands of *Jean Le Taureau* again at the wheel, the more than adequately powerful Bentley sped the intrepid trio the right way back to *Nevers* in optimum time.

However, their mounting excitement became wholly muted after the *Duc* had responded to a message from *Anne* left at the hotel. He telephoned immediately as she had requested. With *une douleur* defying description he informed his two stalwart friends: "*Marie* is missing!"

Chapter Nineteen

Within minutes, the trio were back in the Bentley on their way to *Anne's appartement*. For the first time, *Anne* fell into the *Duc's* outstretched arms and nestled there, savouring brief, welcome, long-absent moments of comfort. But though their bodies had finally come together, yet they remained curiously apart.

Struggle against the notion though she might, the uncomfortable thought that *Marie's* disappearance was in some way due to the appearance in her life of these three men just could not be dispelled, even though she was sure at the deepest level of her being that in no way would any of them harm her daughter, or even wish to!

She decided that, nonetheless, she would be frank, as the *Duc* had been with her. *Théodore de Cornsai-Tantobé* listened to her concerns—as of course he would—with peerless empathy; and even went further—demonstrating his similarly lofty intellect and wisdom—to say that her premiss pointed to the same probable conclusion that he had reached. Laying bare more of what *he* knew, he proposed to her that, unless a freak, unfortunate accident were to explain it, *Marie's* absence almost certainly involved *Mochet*!

"Should I go back to the police and tell them, then?" she asked, her elfin beauty made all the more bewitching by the anguish in her dark, liquid eyes! "They told me to wait twenty-four hours—they said young women sometimes do such things without telling their mothers—but they do not know my *Marie* as I do. She would not treat me so inconsiderately! Now, with what you have told me…"

"I fear the police would treat our suspicions with a great deal of scepticism, no matter how convinced *we* may be. However, *we* know where *M. Mochet* lives—I ascertained that essential knowledge before ever we came to *Nevers*—and the three of us already have experience in dealing with such situations. Let us see what *we* can do."

Despite the misgivings she had voiced, her feminine intuition told *Anne* to put her faith in these men. "Very well," she murmured, "but take care…"

Gloriously, miraculously, all her concerns were to evaporate as she was about to bid farewell to the resolute threesome on the front step of her apartment building.

Crossing the road towards them was her daughter, *Marie!*

"*Oh, Marie, Ma Chérie, c'est merveilleux!* I have been so worried! Where have you been? Where is your scarf?"

Marie smiled at the four, enraptured people before her, but her smile was vacant and distant. "*Maman! Hatch! Monsieur Le Duc! Monsieur Slivovitch!*" Then she staggered a little and shook her head. "*Maman*…I don't remember…"

They led her upstairs, seated her in an armchair and poured her wine. She continued to smile the same, distracted, bewildered smile. It was then that *Alexandrov Slivovitch* noticed the dilation of her pupils!

"*Mademoiselle,* it is possible you may haf suffered some head trauma. Vill you permit me?"

Marie knitted her brows in great concentration, but no memory of the past hours would return. She acquiesced to *Alexandrov Slivovitch's* request.

He carefully inspected her neck and the sides of her face for signs of dried blood, scratches, or contusions. There were none. Then, with his still wholly intact left hand, he gently felt the entire surface of her cranium, but he could find no lumps either.

"*Madame,*" he said to *Anne Laverge,* "has your daughter ever had any psychotic episodes in her life?"

"*Jamais!*"

"Zen I can only conclude she has been drugged! If only I had a syringe and access to a laboratory!"

"I have a syringe," said *Marie* quietly. "I'm a medical researcher. I always carry a kit in my personal belongings."

The noble *Théodore,* who had already grasped his friend's purpose, turned to *Anne Laverge.* "May I use your 'phone, please? I need to make a crucial call!"

"Of course, *Théo,*"—she could not have known the leap his heart gave to hear her use the diminutive of his *prénom*—"it is in the study." She pointed to the door.

The *Duc* returned to a changed *tableau. Hatch* was hunkered next to *Marie,* holding her left hand and benefiting from a gaze of such melting softness the huge American's insides must surely have been shaking like a leaf on a tree. And despite her confused state, *Marie* still had all the golden glory of a newly opened flower! And very nearly, if not already assuredly, she was *Hatch's!* The *Duc* was also certain—as certain as he could be of anything—that *Hatch* would be proud to say that she was his buttercup!

Anne was looking at *Marie* and *Hatch* with an inexpressible poignancy, and then seeing the *Duc,* spontaneously came to him and leant against his side. He gently enveloped her shoulder with his right arm, but could not see the single tear of joy that trickled from her right eye—this was partly because he was on her left side, but it was also down to their height difference, of course, since, in fact, he was well over one metre eighty tall, whereas she was a deceptive one metre sixty, if that; deceptive because her svelte frame and upright, elegant posture made her seem taller than she actually was, even though she always wore flat shoes, but then, of course, it is a truism that appearances can be deceptive, *n'est-ce pas? Mais vous voilà!*

De toute façon…

It would have been entirely explicable if a too-long-suppressed jealous demon had risen like bitter gall in his gullet and caused *Alexandrov Slivovitch* to look on the present *tableau* with homicidal rancour. But no such thing occurred within the chivalrous Ex-Soviet's psyche. He had swabbed and then put a plaster on the needle-prick in *Marie's* right forearm and had sealed the blood sample on which, hopefully, very soon he could work. It was sufficient for him to know that in his own modest way he could put his meagre knowledge to use for the greater good of his friends!

The 'phone rang.

"That will be for me," said the *Duc* in his deep, resonant, wholly individual and seductive baritone.

"*Alexandrov Slivovitch*, you shall have the facilities you require from nine o'clock tomorrow!" he announced upon his return.

"How on earth did you arrange that?" asked an amazed *Anne*.

"Please, do not ask...there are some things I cannot tell...even you!"

"Ah!"

"*Maman, mes amis*, excuse me, but I am very tired..." said *Marie*.

And of course it was agreed the three men would leave so that *Marie* could retire to bed.

Marie was asleep almost as soon as her exquisite head hit her privileged pillow. Sleep, however, eluded *Anne*, in such tumult was she still from the events of the day.

It was for this reason that, at around two in the morning, she heard her daughter speaking. She went quietly to her daughter's room. It was cold. Outside, the temperature had dropped to a perishing fifteen degrees, yet inexplicably, *Marie* had opened the windows and the shutters. Her daughter stood in her cerise night attire before the window frame and *Anne* heard her say: "They have taken a blood sample. One of them, the Russian, will analyse it tomorrow." A pause. "I don't know where." Another pause. "At nine."

"*Marie*," said *Anne*, "who are you talking to?"

Marie at once began to shake, then suddenly became aware of her mother.

"*Maman*, what is it? Oh it's cold! What are you doing here? Why have you opened the windows and shutters?

Anne immediately went to the casement. As she did so, a bat that must have been hanging from the guttering suddenly took flight. *Anne* shuddered and then closed the windows and shutters.

"You must have been sleepwalking, *Ma Chérie*," said the mother reassuringly. "Get back into bed."

Chapter Twenty

"You seem tired, *Anne*," said the *Duc*, his deep, resonant, seductive baritone imbued with a soothing, yet wholly virile, and so in no way equivocal softness.

Anne felt as though she'd been swathed in soft velvet. The *Duc* and *Hatch* had walked to her *appartement* the following morning.

Jean Le Taureau was driving *Alexandrov Slivovitch* to the pharmaceutical laboratory that was now at the Russian's disposal, wholly due to the *Duc's* fortuitous and influential connections. This modern and superbly equipped establishment was some distance out of town in the opposite direction to *Chez Laverge*.

After that, however, the ex-Legionnaire would put other of his skills to very different use. He was to reconnoitre, unseen, the house and grounds where *Mochet* lived.

"I found it difficult to get off to sleep," replied *Anne*, "after…everything, and then *Marie* disturbed me at around two o'clock…she was talking in her sleep and she'd been sleep-walking…so it was an age before *I* finally got off to sleep, but I awoke at my usual time… Ah! The tyranny of habit!"

"How impressive she is," thought the sensitive, cultured aristocrat, "to remain so philosophic in the face of such distress!" And as he looked into the deep, liquid depths of her sleep-deprived eyes, this time he was not wallowing but drowning...though wonderfully so!

"How is *Marie* now?" enquired a concerned *Hatch*.

"She is fine, thank you, *Monsieur*...or may I address you by your *prénom*? *Qu'on se tutoie?*"[33]

The courteous *Hatch* nodded his eager consent.

"I looked in on her ten minutes ago and she was still sleeping soundly. I thought I would let her sleep on."

No sooner had *Anne* said this, however, than *Marie* emerged from her bedroom, delectably draped in a diaphanous *cérise robe de nuit*, through which was gloriously discernable a tasteful, *cérise* ensemble of negligée, bra, and culottes, which only partially covered her voluptuous shoulders, arms, breasts, buttocks, thighs, and calves. The good *Duc* noticed this. As did *Hatch*, of course!

Though *Marie's* almond eyes were still half-glazed with sleep, their deep, liquid depths had never seemed more alluring to the giant American. And how reassured *Hatch* was that she was indeed fully recovered, when she rubbed her exquisitely flat stomach and abdomen and announced she was ready for breakfast.

---

33 "Should we use (the familiar) "tu" with each other?" (Notice how much more succinct the French is. Something, eh?)

After a superb repast, happily, *Hatch* and the *Duc* were able to put aside for a while their pressing problems, the continued contemplation of which could have surely marred their day. Instead, in the company of the flawless *Laverges*, they were shown and savoured the delights of *Nevers*.

Jean Le Taureau returned to *Anne's appartement* at the appointed time and made a report of exemplary, military brevity. *Mochet's* house was isolated. There was cover. There were no guard dogs or alarms. There were two occupants, *Mochet* and a young man.

Jean Le Taureau favoured entry from the rear. Of the two available passageways experience had made him quite sure which one to choose.

Having thanked his doughty major-domo, the *Duc* asked for a description of *Mochet's* companion. At this, the looming ex-Legionnaire suddenly seemed to be made uneasy by the rapt attention of the two women. "I do not know how to put it—*mais alors!* It is *unnatural, Seigneur,* for a man to perm his hair and wear make up, *n'est-ce pas?* And to dress in purple and pink!" A *frisson* shook *Jean's* entire body.

"I see," intoned the shocked nobleman.

"I think we all do, *Théo,*" said *Anne* with charming sensibility. "*Monsieur,*" she continued, "please, may I offer you something after your unpleasant afternoon? And definitely something a little stronger than a *tisane, n'est-ce pas?*"

The burly ex-Legionnaire smiled in sheepish yet deep appreciation. "Perhaps a *calvados, Madame, s'il vous plaît?*"

"*Mais oui!*"

Anne poured a *dose* of the fiery, apple liquor that she judged sufficient for so big a man.

She was a little bemused, however, when with his first *bouchée, Jean Le Taureau* gargled.

Jean looked from the startled *Anne* to the mortified *Duc* and back to the recomposed *Anne.* "*Pardon, Madame! Seigneur!* It was a technique we used after a sandstorm in the desert," he explained, "to remove the nasty taste from our throats. *Milles excuses,* I did it without thinking!"

"*Je vous en prie,*" said his ever-charming hostess. "I understand, *absolument!*"

At half-five, a 'phone call to *Anne's appartement* summoned *Jean Le Taureau* to collect *Alexandrov Slivovitch.* At half-six, they were all enjoying *apéritifs* in the lounge end of the long room that was also diner and kitchen *Chez Laverge.*

"I haf my toxicological results," began the brilliant bio-chemist. "Zhere vere unusual metabolites in *Mademoiselle's* blood. To be brief, ze results almost certainly point to ze recent ingestion of some form of Benzodiazepine!"

"And what is this drug? What does it do?" the hulking American demanded immediately.

"It is mostly harmless; normally a sedative...zis is it's usual use..." Here *Alexandrov Slivovitch* paused. "But it can also enhance one's susceptibility to...hypnotism."

"Which can be used to suppress memory!" added the Duc.

"Indeed, *Mon Cher Théodore*!" agreed *Alexandrov Slivovitch*.

The two women, *Hatch*, and *Jean Le Taureau* gasped at the implications of what they had just heard.

The *Duc* expressed his due appreciation of the Russian, which was duly appreciated…then said with deep, resonant gravity, "It is time we held counsel. It was our original commission simply to recover the chest. However, this has led us to cross the path of *M. Mochet*, whom I am sure has the chest, but whom I am also sure has deliberately sought out the *Laverge* family and abducted, drugged, and most probably hypnotised *Marie*. To what end I still do not know. But I am equally sure it is connected with the chest and its contents. The chest's recovery is now doubly imperative, to prevent its further misuse and to discover *Mochet's* purpose…nay, trebly imperative, also to protect *Marie* from further harm…nay, quadruply imperative, to put an end, once and for all, to *Mochet's* evil machinations, too, for whatever they may be, believe me, evil they most assuredly are!

"What we must do is break into *Mochet's* house and take the chest."

"But," the charming, still innocent *Marie* interjected, "Isn't that against the law? Mightn't it lead to trouble with the police?"

"Indeed, it is against the law, *Marie*—that is *Man's* law…" the corollary of his last comment the *Duc* left tacit…"But I do not think *M. Mochet* will rush to tell our fine *gendarmes* that his stolen goods have themselves been 'stolen!'

"However, I would prefer that, at the very least, *Mochet* himself is not in the house when we make this attempt."

"But I have made an arrangement to meet *M. Mochet* in the library tomorrow morning at ten!" announced the bewitching *Anne*.

Alexandrov Slivovitch, Hatch, Jean Le Taureau, and the *Duc*—but particularly the *Duc*—looked at *Anne* with awed gratitude.

"*Madame,*" said *Alexandrov Slivovitch* with total spontaneity, "I feel both proud and a little humble to know you!" He spoke for them all. *Anne* was wholly, though a little pinkly, gratified.

Immediately thereafter, though—for so fecund was the man's mind—the noble *Duc* cunningly devised an elaborate plan, whereby *Alexandrov Slivovitch* would distract *Mochet's* "companion" and so give time to the *Duc* and *Hatch* to search the house and find and secure the chest. The plan was discussed, refined, and rehearsed, until all were happy with it. And then it was unanimously decided: they would carry it through the following morning!

It is pointless now to relate the details of this plan—subtle, cunning, and elaborate though they were—for reasons that will soon become apparent. Suffice to say, however, that it was subtle, cunning, and elaborate... and *it would have worked!*

The delicious *souper* they all then enjoyed could not wholly dismiss the tense anticipation attendant on the morrow's venture.

The band of conspirators disbanded at ten.

Again, *Anne* slept fitfully, and again she was awoken by sounds emanating from her daughter's room. This time, though she listened, she did not enter. But what she heard chilled her to her marrow!

"*Maman* is meeting you tomorrow morning, *n'est-ce pas?* That is when they will try to gain entry into the house and look for Skerne's chest. The Russian will distract your companion. The other two will search the house…"

Now, in complete reversal of how she was mere seconds before, *Anne* felt suddenly hot and…how exactly could she describe her present state? *Mais oui*—"*bothered*"—*voilà, le mot juste!* She moved immediately to the end of the long room that was also diner and kitchen. She opened the windows and threw back the shutters, so she could breathe more easily. Immediately, she saw an owl, which was perched on the street light opposite her *appartement*, take flight and wing its way into the darkness…*Anne* shuddered and then closed the windows and shutters. Who had her daughter been talking to? The *Duc* should know of this, she decided. If all went well, she would see him tomorrow at noon.

Again, his *incubus* had been disturbed, but *Mochet* felt, nonetheless, that he had learned enough. He kneaded *Marie's* scarf with his podgy, annelid fingers, and a malign smirk distorted his bufonide[34] face. So let them try! He would even play their game! He *would* absent himself and rendezvous with the gullible *Laverge* woman. He would also leave his "companion" in the dark—let each make of the other what they could!

No, he would have a wholly different surprise in store for his visitors! And at this, *Mochet* chuckled a chilling, croaking chuckle.

---

34   The Author would be grateful if anyone could definitely confirm that he has, in fact, coined a new word.

Chapter Twenty-One

The refined French aristocrat and the powerful American astro-physicist were concealed at a suitable vantage point to watch the implementation of the first stage of the *Duc's* cunning, subtle, elaborate, and potentially successful plan—*Alexandrov Slivovitch's* distraction of *Mochet's* Atrocious Acolyte.

A plump youth with a *bouffant* of waved, blonde hair, mascaraed eyelashes, rouged cheeks, and pouting lips opened the front door of *Mochet's* residence to the royal, Russian bio-chemist.

"*Julien Latapette,*" the Quiffed Queer sighed. "And you are?"

"*Alexandrov Slivovitch Romanov.*"

"*Mon, mon! Eh bien, j'irai au pied de nos escaliers!*" While keeping open the door with his right hand—which hung from a wrist that was decidedly limp—with his similarly hung left hand, he smoothed the front of his body-hugging, violet, Shirley Bassey T-shirt and then rubbed his left thigh, which was encased in flesh-gripping, pink jeans. He cast his eye up and down the handicapped, disfigured Russian with growing, impudent disdain.

"And what brings you here, do pray tell me?" he breathed.

"To see *Monsieur Mochet.*"

"And is he expecting you?"

"Possibly."

"Or possibly not. He's just gone out!"

"For long?"

"How should I know?"

"I don't mind waiting."

"Oo, that desperate are we?"

Already the *Duc's* cunning, subtle, and elaborate plan was starting to unravel a tad.[35]

The Noisome Nancy took another sneering look at the once-handsome face of the maimed Muscovite. "Mm, *Monsieur Mochet* must be really slumming it if he's into scarred amputees these days! *Eh bien, chacun à son goût...*I suppose *I* could be of *service*, though I don't think so!" He pouted.

At that moment, a fiend from his subconscious must have seized control of *Alexandrov Slivovitch*, obliterating all else from his thought except blind bitterness and fury! That his misfortunes should be mocked by such a suggestion! He placed the stump of his footless, left leg a little behind him for leverage. He turned the embossed, silver knob at the top of the elegant, cedar-wood cane on which, perforce, he now had to lean, and the thin, razor-sharp, stiletto slid silently from its sheath. With nary a scruple, he jabbed the botulinum-impregnated blade into the right buttock of this Monstrous Abomination, this Hideous Insult to the Creator's Divine Design.

Paused primarily by perplexity and pain, the Pierced Pervert's posterior was presently paralysed by the poison from the perpetrator's poignard!

Still driven by this incandescent ire from his Id, the Ex-Soviet then tilted and turned the embossed silver

---

35   Or an iota or a smidgeon...

knob and squirted a jet of concentrated hydrofluoric acid onto the left shoe of the Degenerate Jessie.

Unable now to move his whole right leg, *Julien Latapette* was nonetheless able to look down at one of the pair of his favourite shoes, as it started to smoke and disintegrate. Still with feeling in his left foot, his first sensation was one of cold. But, as the supremely caustic chemical ate into skin and flesh and began its inexorable corrosion of the bones of his foot, the Pitiable Ponce keened in horrific agony. His face contorted into a hideous grimace.

Seeing this, and still wholly in the grip of hitherto repressed rage, *Alexandrov Slivovitch* relished again unsheathing and raising his envenomed stiletto to prick with the most exquisite precision the rouged cheek of this Preening Primrose. Now that grimace would be frozen there for weeks. Would this Simpering Sodomite be of "service" to *anyone* anytime soon? *Alexandrov Slivovitch* didn't think so!

Alexandrov Slivovitch slowly regained calm. As he did so, he ruefully wondered how His Maker might judge what he had just done? (His supreme act of defection from the Soviet Regime, after all, had been to embrace the reviled religion of Rome!)

But then, he recalled that the All-Knowing Father had once wiped out the inhabitants of two entire cities to punish the very same vice that this Big Girl's Blouse so flagrantly flaunted! And in His day, hadn't even Jesus, His Divine Son, been all for kicking shit out of those bankers[36] in the temple? So, he felt then that,

---

36   An example of yet another culture that invented rhyming slang!

yes, actually, The Almighty would probably be quietly approving! After all, what a Rampant Pufta *Latapette* clearly was! So, in fact, if anything, the Putrid Piece Of Work had got off lightly! *Alexandrov Slivovitch* was then gratified that, probably, in his own, small way, he had also been merciful in his pursuance of God's Supreme Purpose!

Alexandrov Slivovitch was suddenly overwhelmed, too, with regret that he had deviated completely from the *Duc's* carefully laid plan…until he saw—in a trice— that he had *not* deviated a jot from its aim! If anything, their task was now simpler.

This was what the *Duc* also quickly deduced, after he and *Hatch* had raced in some perturbation from their concealed vantage point to the scene of their comrade's inexplicable aberration.

Thus, that superior and subtle intellect was even able to reflect that, in the Mysterious Ways In Which God works, so often what at first sight seems an apparent, if lesser evil, paradoxically proves to be part of a greater good in His Ineffable Plan…

One glance at the state of the supine figure told the *Duc* that any threat this Horrid Abhorrence might have posed was now non-existent. "Get back to the car, *Alexandrov*! If *Mochet* returns, distract him!"

The first thing the *Duc* noticed as he and *Hatch* entered the hall was *Marie's* scarf hanging from a hook on the wall. The *Duc* wondered what its value to *Mochet*

might be, and though tempted to pluck it there and then and return it to its delightful owner, his instinct told him that to leave it might serve a higher end...and so leave it he did.

Urgently, the duo scoured the innards of the house. They found nothing, until they discovered a lumber-room at its farthermost reaches. And in it were chests, lots of them, of all different shapes and sizes.

The *Duc* reflected for a mere instant then smiled. "*Hatch*," he asked, "where do you hide a book?"

"Whar do yer hide a book?" the huge American repeated, for a moment at a loss. Why was the good *Duc* asking him, and now of all moments, where to hide a book? Then light dawned. "Lawdy, lawdy! Wha, 'course! In a library! Har's whar he's hidden the chest! But thar's fifty'o mo! So which one is it? Wha, the cunning coyote!"

But the *Duc's* arcane, painstakingly acquired knowledge had already led him to narrow the field. He had seen the symbols marked on the floor beneath a single, nondescript chest and knew immediately the purpose of those markings. This was surely the prize they sought...*Mochet* had seriously underestimated the adversary with whom he was engaged.

The *Duc* knew, though, that now *he* had to proceed with extreme caution. Yet he was ready. He lifted from around his neck the crucifix and chain made of the noblest of all metals, which he always wore, and advanced trepidly towards his goal. His hand reached with infinite caution across the perimeter of the symbols. He turned the verdigris-covered key and gingerly lifted the chest's lid.

Their search was indeed at an end! Inside were two vellum scrolls, yellowed with age and bound by leather thongs, and between them a golden artefact. It had been cast in the exact shape of a life-size[37], proudly erect, male member.

But at once, the place grew dark and chill, and what seemed like motes of incandescent dust began to swirl above the chest. The *Duc* stepped backwards and watched, his hand all the while clutching his golden cross.

Slowly, something was taking bodily form on the fallen lid of the chest; something that both men failed to recognise immediately! But it was *Hatch* who finally knew. It was due to a sojourn he'd taken, after his return from 'Nam', on the intriguing island of Madagascar. Now fully formed and ensconced on the lid of the chest was an *Aye-Aye*—that *Nosferatu* of the lemur world—and it was starting to grow in size! Eventually, it was as tall as *Hatch* himself, the contents of whose large intestine were close to deliquescent even as he watched. The beast's ghoulish, red eyes regarded them both balefully, and it waved threateningly its freakish, protracted finger with that long, barbarous nail.

But the magnificent *Duc* was undaunted and wholly prepared! He raised his crucifix and advanced on the monstrosity as he intoned something known to very few, even among the Adept. Alone, the words were potent against the greatest of evils, but when conjoined with that glorious symbol of Man's Salvation, they were invincible!

---

37   Its size was close to the upper end of the range…not, of course, that it matters!

> *"Quem spectas?*
> *Buccam pugni desideras?*
> *Dentes tuos custodire amare habebas?"*[38]

"You bastard! You bastard!" gibbered the spectre, but even as it did so, both sound and sight were fading. Within thirty seconds, the abominable apparition was wholly gone.

"*Hatch*, grab the chest and let's get out of here!"

As resolidification of the content of his bowels was now occurring, *Hatch* needed no second bidding. He seized the chest and, within a minute, it was in the boot of the Bentley, which was whisking them all away, the car's more than adequate power never more appreciated than now!

Yet the apparition had confirmed the *Duc's* gravest suspicion—this *Mochet* must be an Adept of the left-hand path, equal in prowess to *him*! How else could such a hideous phantasm be given corporeal form during the hours of daylight?

So, what would tip the balance in the contest that the two now faced? The *Duc* was reassured at once when he reflected that the difference lay in which master they each served! Though he could not allow himself even a quark of complacency, and he would have to deploy all his knowledge, cunning, wit, and courage to outplay this foe, the *Duc* remained confident that, ultimately, he must prevail!

---

38   See the Glossary.

The Talisman of Skerne   by Tom Carr

The undaunted Duc confronts that Nosferatu of the lemur world – the Aye-Aye…

One glance at *Julien Latapette* would have revealed to the meanest intelligence that something untoward had occurred. *M. Mochet's* intelligence was in no way mean, however, so in other ways *he* might be! He was already musing as to what should be done about his "companion" as he hastened to check on his first priority!

He had to lean against the doorjamb of the lumber-room as the implications of the chest's removal impinged upon him. Not only was his carefully laid plan in serious jeopardy, but also he realised now that he must be facing an adversary that he had seriously underestimated!

True, he had the medium of the *Laverge* girl still... and he could now barely wait for nightfall to learn what she knew. But what he had thought would be a simple, almost *blasé* ruse to eavesdrop on these people could now turn out to be more like a game of chess played at the highest level!

Which one of the three of them was the *Ipsissimus?* For only such an Adept could have had the means to thwart the *Aye-Aye!* It was surely *Monsieur Le Duc,* the other two were too young to have yet scaled such a pinnacle!

For this person, *Mochet* was at once possessed by an all-consuming hatred. His toad-like body was stricken by an impotent, seething wrath.

This no doubt informed the decision he now made. *Latapette's* left foot clearly needed amputation. This would bring in its wake unwanted scrutiny and awkward questions! For how ever long the facial paralysis lasted, the Feckless Fairy would also require either tube-feeding or intravenous nourishment, too...and *Mochet* was already tiring of the *Mincing Mary-Ann!* When *Mochet* had plucked him from the streets of *Marseilles, Latapette* was a "missing person"—although not missed! He had long been disowned by an outraged *fonctionnaire* of a father who was also a parish dignitary. So, in fact, *Julien's* status would not change, simply his state!

Mochet went from the lumber-room to his study and took a pistol and silencer from his desk draw.

Julien's eyes pleaded pitiably, as he lay stricken on the hall floor, his face frozen in its grimace, the remains of his left foot still smoking. *Mochet* smiled at him reassuringly and then shot him in the head.

Digging a grave and cleaning the floor would be welcome physical distraction from the mental and emotional turmoil with which *Mochet* was now beset!

Chapter Twenty-Two

The triumphant triumvirate arrived at *Anne's appartement* just after noon. Aware as he was, now, of the probable magnitude of *Mochet's* malevolence, the *Duc* had decided that they must remove themselves and their prize at once from the vicinity of this Malicious Monster, so their suitcases were already in the Bentley's capacious boot, next to Skerne's chest.

But could the *Duc* convince the two *Laverges* of the real nature of the danger *they* faced, and persuade *them*, too, to leave, as he knew indeed they should?

He could not simply rely, he realised, on the deep, resonant, seductive delivery of his arguments but, crucially, on the cogency of the arguments themselves!

"*Eh bien*," he began with measured, baritonal *gravitas*, as he faced the two winsome women and mustered all his rhetoric. "Do you want to come back to my place!"

There was a pregnant pause, the pregnancy of which, though, was for the *Duc* close to unbearable!

"*Théo*," responded *Anne* finally. "Are you asking *Marie* and myself to suddenly 'up sticks' and spend the rest of our summer *congé*[39] in a *château* in the south of France?"

The *Duc* decided he must be totally frank. "*Oui*," he said.

"*Marie*, what do you think?" Mother and daughter exchanged a look the *Duc* could not interpret.

---

39   Congé—leave

Both women looked at each other, pouting lips, raising eyebrows, and shrugging shoulders—that quintessential yet strangely charming, French way *les Françaises* have of being coquettish!

"*Mais allons-y!* " said *Marie.*

And so, within an hour, they were all on the road. The urgency of putting distance between themselves and *Mochet* was very soon replaced by the realisation that they had not yet eaten. They dined simply, yet well, at a roadside, rural *auberge.* Three hours later, they were again *en route.*

The logistics imposed by the Bentley placed the hulking *Hatch* up front, beside the similarly chunky *chauffeur,* while the sumptuous, leather back seat comfortably accommodated the slim *Alexandrov Slivovitch,* the svelte *Laverges* and the lithe *Duc.* However, the rear seat was still not sufficiently spacious to prevent thigh contact between *Anne* and the *Duc.* This constant *frottage* resulted around *Clermond-Ferrand* in the *Duc* having an erection so rampant it would have eclipsed Skerne's Talisman itself! Debarred from using nettles to flagellate his renegade todger into chaste submission, the *Duc* deployed another technique—dwelling mentally on the attributes of seriously unappealing females—Medusa The Gorgon, Rosa Kleb,[40] Margaret Thatcher[41] —but even so, his willy waxed and waned all the way to *Millau,* because *Anne's* lively conversation

40   See "From Russia With Love."
41   This is 1976. The good Duc, an astute student of International Politics, had already followed this lady's first months as leader of the British Tory Party. He thought her likely to become the United Kingdom's first woman Prime Minister. It would be a slight upon the Duc's breeding—and indeed upon the lady herself—to suggest

constantly distracted him and also the *frottage* was sublimely unrelenting!

Having wrestled the bulky vehicle round the endless hairpins to the bottom of *Les Gorges Du Tarn*, and squeezed its considerable size through the narrow streets of that small and pleasant town that was nonetheless France's most notorious bottleneck, *Jean Le Taureau* was relieved when the *Duc* suggested a *restoratif* before they began the equally tortuous assent up the southern wall of the valley. As he savoured his first *bouchée* of the local *eau de vie*, *Jean Le Taureau* mused whimsically: "If only some clever bastards could build a viaduct across this valley, why, it would take easily two hours off the time of the journey...eh bien, maybe someday..." He took a second *bouchée* of *eau de vie*, excused himself from the rest of the party, and strolled to the shade of a nearby tree and lit a calming *Gauloise*...

⁕

The *Duc* had 'phoned his French housekeeper from *Anne's appartement* minutes before they left. *Mathilde Lasage* now awaited the arrival of his two new guests with a mixture of anticipation and dread. Though housekeeping was indeed her function in *Le Château*, altogether greater had been and still was her *rôle* in the *Duc's* life.

Mathilde had been widowed shortly after the onset of the Second World War at the young age of twenty-four. With her young infant of seven months, she had

---

that the Duc had already deemed her a strident harpy. *Non!* Better to say that, *tout simplement*, she was not wholly to his taste...

fled her native Normandy to the relative safety of the then unoccupied *Midi* and the refuge of her cousin's presbytery. Her priestly relative had spoken to his two most prestigious parishioners, the now, sadly, deceased parents of the present *Duc*, who were happy to give *Mathilde* employment in their household. *Théodore De Cornsai-Tantobé* was then just a young boy of six.

A bond formed between the young *Normande* and the *Duc*-to-be, who fetched and carried for her in the kitchen, filled baskets for her with the produce of the orchards and gardens, and played with her young son[42] as he grew. She had effectively been, first, his *Nounou*, but later also his *Guide* and *Confidante* and surrogate *Maman!* To his great good fortune, the *Duc* had had—due to this happy association—all the benefits of Norman wisdom since his earliest childhood! They continued to this day!

And how *Mathilde* had longed that *Le Château* would one day have again a *Châtelaine*. This—amongst other things—because she craved someone she could converse with *sensibly* about the colour of new curtains, new towels, new bed sheets (she was sick of taupe), wallpaper, flower arrangements, menus, and the layout of the gardens.

---

42   The *Duc* and *Sébastian* remain good friends to this day. *Sébastian* is a now a *viticulteur* of renown in the region.

... "if only some clever bastards could build a viaduct across this valley"...

Once described in her youth by the envious, local "bucks"—when she had finally chosen her "beau"—as *une jeune fille vive*[43], *Mathilde* had long since passed through the first two of the three stages of womanhood—horses, hormones, and horticulture...How lovely it would be to have someone with whom she could share her passion for gardens!

But what if they did not "get on?"

And she had to admit, she also felt something akin to that tad-smidgeon-iota of jealousy every woman feels for a daughter-in-law! As she had when her *Sébastian* married his *Carole*...

Didier Bénitier, still the local *curé*—indeed it was he who had baptised the infant *Duc*—was enjoying a glass of *vin rouge* with his cousin in *Le Château's* kitchen when the party arrived. *Didier* was a man of generous nature but volatile temper. To befit his station, he had disciplined his impulse to swear frequently at members of his congregation by training himself to substitute other, innocuous words that shared the same initial sound as the profanity. His academic discipline had been Chemistry, so he had chosen the names of elements from the Periodic Table.

"*Phosphorus Helium!*" he exclaimed, when he realised the *Duc* was home. "I'll shift my *Argon* out of here shortly and leave the place free for *Théodore* and his guests.

---

43   "Spirited filly."

Now, *Mathilde,* don't go being an interfering *Bismuth* and *Cobalt* everything up! "

"Get away with you," explained *Mathilde Lasage* with great sagacity.

However, *Didier* lingered awhile outside *Le Château's* two magnificent chestnut wood front portals to greet the *Duc, Hatch,* and *Alexandrov Slivovitch* and to meet the two well-favoured women who immediately made on him an impression that was—well—favourable!

As *Didier Bénitier* left, he reflected that the sins of impurity the *Duc* would now confide to him in the confessional were much less likely to be with himself than with another! That would warrant *two* decades of the rosary for his penance—but so what? The lucky *Barium!* When he realised that he, too, was having prurient thoughts, the good *curé* blessed himself and made a pious ejaculation.

Pleased as he was to introduce *Anne* and *Marie* to his friend and confessor, the *Duc* now led the two women— and indeed one in particular—to a meeting that was much more portentous!

Chapter Twenty-three

Certain conjunctions in history have been seminal— *Chamberlain's* meeting with *Hitler*, *Churchill's* meeting with *Stalin*, and *Clay's*[44] first fight with *Liston* for the Heavyweight Championship of the World!

Such would the meeting of *Anne* and *Mathilde* also prove to be!

The *Duc* and his entourage entered *Le Château Du Prat Ragé's* capacious, rustic kitchen. Emerging through the bunches of herbs and garlic bulbs hanging from hooks in the ceiling beams appeared *Mathilde* with whom at once the *Duc*, *Hatch*, and *Alexandrov Slivovitch* exchanged affectionate—though wholly chaste— *bisous*[45].

First round, *Mathilde!*

"*Mathilde*, let me present to you *Anne* and *Marie Laverge*."

The expected, polite exchanges were politely exchanged. *Mathilde* was impressed by, but also felt a tad-smidgeon-iota of disquiet because of the arresting beauty of the two women. Both daughter *and* mother could ensnare any man...should she detect an iota-

---

44   As Mohammed Ali was known at the time.

45   "Kisses"—this renowned French custom is delightful, but at large social gatherings can sometimes take up a huge chunk of the event...happily, though, not the case here.

smidgeon-tad[46] of guile in their involvement with the *Duc* and *Hatch*, then "woe betide!"[47]

Mathilde shades the second round!

But *Mathilde* had also heard the flawless BBC French both daughter and mother spoke with such charming *douceur.*

Third round, *Anne!*

En plus, as she learned of their qualifications and employment, she admitted that maybe the *Duc's* judgement was sound.

Fourth round, *Anne!*

"*Madame*, do you have a garden?"

"*Non, hélas*, I live in an *appartement*..."

At the start of the fifth, *Anne* is suddenly unable to see her way forward. "But as needs must...I am divorced— still, with careful thought about *décor*, one can transform even so restricted an environment, *n'est-ce pas?* I love pitting my wits against challenges like that..."

She survives by a superb, evasive retreat, worthy of *Cassius* himself or even, dare it be said, *Jack Johnson*, until her vision starts to clear...

"...and also my ex-husband is a very talented garden designer—I learned so much from him! I do miss having a garden..."

Going into the sixth, *Anne* now moves onto the offensive. "*Théodore* has talked to me about your cooking and your splendid kitchen-garden. I look forward, if I may, to learning some of your recipes...I love cooking...

---

46   The Author is still uncertain of the rank order.

47   Indeed, also the Author's own mother's most harrowing admonition..."Now, woe betide, Our Tommy!" (Shudder).

maybe while I'm here, could I perhaps help and watch and learn, please, *Madame?* And of course, see the garden?"

Mathilde stays in her corner at the start of the seventh!

So indeed, *Mathilde* is *Liston* to *Anne's Clay*, but unlike *Sonny's* surrender, hers is wholly a happy one!

"I've put together" *Mathilde* announced, "a little, light *souper*: ham and melon with *muscat comme hors d'oeuvres*. Then cold, roast quail, *salade mixte avec une vinaigrette* and cold, diced *pommes de terre* with *aïoli* and chives. There is also cheese and fruit. *Théodore* let me know in advance his choice of wine.

"But let me show you first to your rooms. You will want to freshen up, of course. But then, s*ervez-vous et bon appétit!* *Madame*, if you wish, I'll show you round the kitchen garden after breakfast tomorrow morning..."

And, as *Anne's* response was an enthusiastic affirmative—which of course it would be—a short while later *Mathilde* took a most contented leave.

Sometime after that, the *Duc* led guests even more fragrant, if possible, than *Mary Archer* to the meal, which was spread on the exquisite, taupe, linen tablecloths covering the enormous, highly polished olive wood table at the centre of *Le Château's* imposing *salle de banquet*.

At the *Duc's* prior request, *Mathilde* had indeed decanted a bottle of vintage 1956 *Départdieu-Belmondo* rouge—a *Carignan-Syrah assemblage*, a particular favourite of the *Duc*, the superior refinement of whose taste was renowned.[48] Certain the wine would now be perfectly *chambré*, he poured a little of the velvety, dark liquid into an exquisite, antique, ovoid, cut-glass goblet, which bore by means of subtle etching his family emblem, swirled the wine expertly, first to see its "*couleur*," then test its "*bouquet*," before taking a "*bouchée*," which he savoured with that expert, buccal dexterity that *Anne* could not fail to admire (or anticipate). Finally, he swallowed and announced to his guests in his deep, resonant, seductive, and wholly individual baritone, "I think you will appreciate this; it is ...feline without being in the least predatory!"

His guests voiced their thanks as their exquisite, antique, ovoid, cut-glass goblets were charged. These vessels also bore by means of subtle etching the *Duc's* family emblem, an heirloom his two new guests had simultaneously yet independently deduced with incisive insight! Upon taking *their* first *bouchées*, all four guests also simultaneously yet independently reflected how apt indeed had been the *Duc's* appraisal of the wine!

It was the perfect accompaniment to a splendid meal. Something else was almost palpable too...that in every respect there was just so much harmony in that room!

Though the *quinze août* had come and gone, nevertheless it felt to the five *arrivés* that they had stepped back into summer. After their meal, both *Anne* and the

---

48   Throughout the wine-tasting world!

Duc and *Marie* and *Hatch* ventured into the magnificent grounds of *Le Château*. The noble *Duc's* ancestral home was superbly situated on the cusp between the coastal plains of the *Languedoc* and the foothills of *Le Massif Central*. The evening warmth enfolded each couple like a caress, the air was electric with the trilling of myriad *cigales* and, in the gloaming, the surrounding *paysage*—so luminous during the day—was a muted canvas of near-mystical azure. Mm!

Now, wholly at ease with the world, *Anne* finally told the *Duc* about *Marie's* odd, nocturnal behaviour of the previous two nights.

The *Duc* listened with growing concern; but also—with a phlegm that was almost Britannic—he managed to convey none of this to his delightful companion.

"*Anne*, may I ask you, were there any...animals nearby, did you notice?"

"*Mon Dieu, mais oui*, there was a bat on the first night outside *Marie's* window, and an owl on the second..."

"*Mochet's incubi*," murmured the *Duc* before he could prevent himself.

"*Théo*, what do you know...what aren't you telling me?"

She was both too intelligent and also now too dear to him to deceive. So much for his phlegm! He would have to cough up everything to her!

"*Anne*, I've been afraid that, if I confided my suspicions to you, at best you would laugh at them, at worst you would think I was mad...and our relationship would be in peril..."

"*Théo*, you must tell me!" And the look of anguish on her adorable face was torment to his soul.

"*Eh bien!* Where do I begin?" For a moment, the noble *Duc* paused, a crease furrowed his distinguished forehead, and his brows knitted in great concentration. To *Anne*, he had never seemed as stalwart or dependable as he did now!

"*Alors*," he began, "the drama of *Marie's* disappearance and return, the swiftness with which events have moved since…and, indeed, the few stolen hours of enjoyment in between, have meant that I have not yet related to you what I gleaned from your ex-husband. Before ever *Mochet* came to *Nevers*, he had sought out your husband in *Chinon*. Then he comes to *Nevers* and seeks *you* out, too. And I'm totally convinced, after what you have just told me, that *Mochet* abducted *Marie*, drugged and hypnotised her, and then allowed her back into our fold."

"But *why?*"

"Because I believe your family is important to him in some way. I believe this importance is somehow connected to the contents of Skerne's chest and also… to an odd coincidence, loath though I am…loath though we both are, to admit to them…*Anne*, has it ever occurred to you that *Anne, Joachim,* and *Marie*…Anna, Joachim, and Mary…were the names of members of another family?"

"*Mais oui!* My mother made such a deal of it when we named *Marie*. She called us for a while 'The Holy Family!' How wrong she was!" *Anne* smiled a smile that was more rueful than bitter. "But surely," she continued, "this cannot be the basis of *Mochet's*…*Mochet's* what?"

"*Mochet's evil!*" murmured the *Duc.*

"But what does he want of us? What is he up to?"

"That I still don't know. But tomorrow, I am going beyond the bounds of my commission. I am going to scrutinise the contents of Skerne's chest. That is where we will find the answer, I am certain!"

The two fell silent for a while, walked on together through *Le Château's* superb grounds, and appreciated the panorama all over again in what remained of the light.

"*Théo,*" said *Anne* presently. "What do you know about *Marie's* recent nighttime behaviour?"

The sudden constriction of the good *Duc's* throat rendered him speechless for several seconds. "Know?" he finally murmured. "I know nothing for certain."

"Then suspect?"

Again, he was speechless for some moments. "*Anne,* I had hoped that we might not need to go there yet… this is the moment I have most feared. But because I wish to keep nothing from you, I will tell you…even though, after what I am about to say, you will probably tell me I must be mad."

"Try me!"

"*Eh bien.* What I happen to know from my own research, what *Hatch* and I certainly learned from our experiences in that house this morning, all point to the fact that *Mochet* is a considerable adept in the practices of the Left-hand Path…what is popularly known as Black Magic. I am sure *Marie* has been made his unwitting spy. Each animal she speaks to at night is, in fact, one of *Mochet's incubi,* the medium through which he learns

what she has to tell him about us, our movements, and
our intentions."

"*Théo*, do you seriously believe this? You must be
mad!"

Chapter Twenty-four

At once both—as the evening immediately lost for either something of its magic—regretted the words each had just uttered. An aching at the very depths of their souls afflicted the *Duc* and *Anne* in equal measure, as they mentally confronted the barrier that had, unbidden, sprung up suddenly between them. Each sought desperately for the means to breech it.

To the *Duc*, this was also evidence of *Mochet's* malignity! His thought reinforced his determination *not* to use *his* powers as an Adept, even to dispel *Anne's* doubts. Never could he wittingly expose her to horrors it were better she did not know existed! Yet the very same notion also gave him a glimmer of hope…Perhaps there were lesser "phenomena" she *could* see that would accomplish the same end!

"*Anne*," he said presently. "Those shutters there"—he pointed to a casement on the first floor of the facing wall of the *château*—"are those of *Marie's* bedroom. After what you have told me, I intend to keep vigil here tonight. These 'occurrences' have occurred in the very early hours, *oui*? If you are not too tired, and would still like to stay with me to observe what happens. Perhaps that may soften your scepticism a little. Please."

It was testament to her openness of mind—and of course to her feelings for the *Duc*, too—that *Anne* agreed.

First, however, the two went inside to spend the final part of the evening with the others.

∞✲∞

Alexandrov Slivovitch and *Jean Le Taureau* had just finished another chess lesson. *Alexandrov Slivovitch* was toasting his pupil with *vodka*; *Jean* was toasting his teacher with *calvados*. But *Jean* had that day conceived an even greater admiration for his talented tutor—he wholly approved of the biblical retribution *Alexandrov Slivovitch* had meted out earlier to the *Perfumed Pansy*!

Alexandrov Slivovitch's view of his own behaviour, on the other hand, was somewhat different—but of that, more later.

∞✲∞

Hatch and *Marie* had also re-entered *Le Château* but presently had eyes only for each other.

So, it is unsurprising that the muscular American should be wholly dismayed and bewildered when, at midnight, the bewitching *Marie* peremptorily removed herself from his presence with a curt goodnight and nary a backward glance.

The two well-toasted chess-players also took to their respective rooms about the same time, and even *Anne* and the *Duc* parted company for brief moments, as each went to find an extra layer of clothing…and the *Duc* to avail himself of something else far more pursuant to his purpose.

But shortly afterwards, they were reunited in the garden and began their watch. Nor had they long to wait.

Perhaps half-an-hour after she had so curtly quit *Hatch's* company, *Marie* opened the windows and shutters of her bedroom. She was wearing her diaphanous *robe de nuit*, through which, though, because of the dark, the *Duc* could *not* discern her tasteful, *cérise* ensemble of negligée, bra, and culottes, which only partially covered her voluptuous shoulders, arms, breasts, buttocks, thighs, and calves. Indeed, she may have been wearing nothing else at all...fortunately, at that moment, the *Duc* reflected, as other wise heads have, that if he took all the girls he knew when he was single and put them all together for one night, they'd still not match his sweet imagination...so on that faculty, he now put an immediate curb!

Marie stood rigid and stared trance-like at the tree directly before her, which was scarcely five metres from *Le Château's* wall.

From the obscurity of his hiding place nearby, the *Duc* stared with his noble, piercing, dark eyes into the foliage of the majestic conifer, and at first, could see nothing. But, presently, he perceived the glint of two oval, close-set eyes and thereafter the outline—a deeper blackness amid the arboreal dark—of a cat stretched along the branch closest to *Marie*!

Using his long, aristocratic right forefinger at the end of which was an impeccably manicured nail, the noble *Duc* first enjoined *Anne* to silence by placing his digit across his perfectly proportioned lips, then directed her gaze to *Mochet's incubus,* by using the same superlative index to point—a movement which, though, under the circumstances, was in no way rude!

And it was, at that very moment, that *Marie* began to speak!

"Where are we? We are at the *Duc's* home." A pause during which *Marie* appeared attentive. "It is called *Le Château du Prat Ragé*—it is between *Narbonne* and *Béziers.*" Another attentive pause. "Yes, the Talisman and its chest are here, but I don't know where. Somewhere in the house, I suppose." Again *Marie* seemed to be listening to an inaudible interlocutor. "Yes, I will try and find out tomorrow." And again she seemed to listen. "I do not know the *Duc's* purpose in taking the Talisman. And no, I have had no carnal knowledge of the American. I am keeping myself intact, as you instructed…I realise my body is destined for a higher purpose…"

Anne could barely stifle a cry. The *Duc* seized the moment. He took from his pocket a ceramic phial, removed its stopper and hurled its contents at the thing on the branch. Mercury and Salt, that ancient, proven elixir against all evil—the *Duc* always had some in his bedroom in case of just such an emergency.

"Look!" he cried to *Anne,* as his projectile reached its target. *Mochet's* minion faded from sight, and in the air hung a plaintive wail, as of a cat that had been scalded.

Previously, without the sensible and true avouch of her own eyes, even if she had read this in a book, *Anne* would have dismissed it as silly, implausible nonsense! *Mais maintenant! Alors!*

She looked at the *Duc* with renewed, indeed with even greater respect and admiration, and a profound contrition too.

"*Théo,* I am so sorry for doubting you…sorry for what I said!"

"*Anne!* *Non!* *Non!* Your doubts…did your intellect credit…though we were at odds, to me you were still wholly admirable!" And the elated aristocrat held out his arms to this adorable woman who had wholly captured his heart. She took his slender, aristocratic fingers at the ends of which were superbly manicured nails in her own equally elegant hands and moved towards him. Within the blink of an eye, they were in each other's arms and their lips conjoined in an osculation that was long overdue!

At that moment, *Marie* emerged from her trance.

"*Oh non!* *Maman!* *Théodore!* *S'il vous plaît!*" she exclaimed. "*C'est trop!* *Faîtes-le ailleurs!*"[49]

---

49   Oh no! Mum! *Théodore!* Please! It's too much! Do it somewhere else!

Chapter Twenty-five

For rapturous seconds before *Marie* spoke, the *Duc* had been in a state of sublime oblivion. Then, for the briefest moment, with an uncharacteristic—though in this case—wholly understandable lapse of beneficence, his soul's plaintive plea had been, *Don't! Don't leave my embrace, for here in my arms is your place...don't...please don't!* But the noble *Duc* had as quickly regained composure and was thankful, then, that he had not voiced his feelings, for in no way would he wish ever again to embarrass or upset either woman. Moreover, he now knew that he must waste no more time in learning the secrets of Skerne's chest, even if it meant another night would pass before he and *Anne* would see if things might...go further! A whole night maybe without sleeping, working till the morning came creeping!

The *Duc* explained to *Anne* his immediate intentions. She confessed she was overcome by everything that had happened over the past days and felt suddenly very tired. And she wholly understood now the urgency of what he had to do. Yet he saw, nonetheless, to his great joy, a slight but most definite *moue* of disappointment on her face!

Quand même!

The *Duc* and *Anne* went through the green door that led back into the *salle de banquet*, passing the old piano there, and exiting through an identical door at

197

the other end of the room into the majestic entrance hall. Together, they mounted the chateau's magnificent sweeping staircase.

After agreeing they would say nothing yet to *Marie* about the strange words she had uttered into the night, the two stole another brief kiss, and then parted.

Skerne's chest was in the *Duc's* bedroom. He carried it to the superb, mahogany *Louis XV escritoire* that was in the corner of the adjoining antechamber. Before reopening the nondescript box, he went to the exquisite, antique, ovoid, cut-glass decanter, which bore by means of subtle etching his family emblem, and poured into the equally antique, exquisite, ovoid, cut-glass brandy glass, which also bore by means of subtle etching his family emblem—the two *objets d'art* (for how could they *not* merit that term) were now always at his bedside—a glass of vintage *Cerdan-Carpentier armagnac*. This would give him the requisite sustenance for the cerebral undertaking that was now at hand!

Gingerly, he first removed the Talisman from the chest. He gently manipulated the phallus with the forefinger and thumb of each long, aristocratic, well-manicured, experienced hand in order to inspect its every aspect. It was indeed of enviable proportions, and its verisimilitude... *mais vraiment*! But on closer study, he noticed in the surface of the gold, a few faint scratches and blemishes that had accrued over the centuries.

Next, with the utmost care, he removed the two vellum scrolls and unbound them. Both were yellowed with age and creased and split in various places, but the text—written in ink—was almost wholly legible. It was in

Latin. Translating it would be for the *Duc* a pleasurable challenge the scholarly aristocrat had not savoured for some time.

How different, though, were his feelings when he had finished! The terrible import of the scrolls had wholly blunted any appreciation he would surely otherwise have had of the author's subtle use of the ablative absolute!

The *Duc* finished his task even as the morning sun began to dapple the surrounding hills with its damask glow. Utterly exhausted now, *Théodore de Cornsai-Tantobé* sprawled onto the delicate, taupe, linen sheets draped over his ancestral bed and mercifully sank into a few hours of deep, essential sleep...essential, for he still had to divine *Mochet's* ultimate purpose, though dire suspicions had already entered his head, and he needed to devise a counter-strategy...all of which required a fresh mind!

The others, too, were late to rise and, so, the *Duc* was able to join them before they breakfasted. *Mathilde* was in no way perturbed—the yoghurts, clotted cream, milk, and divers fruit juices could be brought from the fridge at any time. The cereals and fruits of various kinds were already on the table; the *Duc* and his guests could partake of them when they wished; and the *croissants, pains au chocolat,* and the omelettes and *crêpes* favoured by both the American and the Russian would remain deliciously hot in the luxurious, silver chafing dishes ranged along the room's exquisite and imposing olive wood sideboard. Once the meal had started, *Mathilde* could then time to perfection the percolation of the rare *Moreno-Chakiris* Costa Rican coffee—the noble *Duc's* personal favourite!

Before they were all *à table*, the unpresumptuous *Duc* made his customary visit to the kitchen to thank *Mathilde*, and so was also able to ask her if she would include *Marie* in the invitation she would soon repeat to *Anne* to look round the kitchen garden after they had eaten.

When the final bowls of coffee were drained, *Mathilde* came immediately into the magnificent *salle de banquet* and said, "*Madame*, would you like to see the kitchen garden now? And *Mademoiselle*, it would please me a great deal if I could show you it too?"

Thus, the *Duc* had gained some time alone with *Hatch* to explain matters.

And, indeed, it was initially a relief to *Hatch* to have matters explained! He had been totally bemused to rediscover a *Marie*, as intimate and affectionate in the morning, as she had been so suddenly aloof and dismissive at midnight! But his relief was quickly replaced by a growing anger, as he fully grasped what the *Duc* had told him.

"*Ne t'inquiète pas, mon brave!*"[50] reassured the wise aristocrat, his tone suffused with a profound though wholly chaste love for his young friend, "I have the means to release *Marie* from this Fiend's clutches, but I cannot do so until our plans are fully formed. In the meantime,

---

50   Calm down, my dear.

we must not say in front of *Marie* anything we do not wish *Mochet* to know. Undoubtedly, she has already—through no fault of her own—told this Demon much about us, but there is much he still does not know, much about which he is still uncertain. That is to our advantage, an advantage we must do all in our power to maintain!

"*Hatch, mon cher ami*, I will give you the use of the *Bugatti*. Today, whisk *Marie* away into our lovely region, show her the sights, wine and dine her...enjoy your time together...

"That will give the rest of us the freedom to plan and act without restraint. You will learn what we're about, later, just after midnight when she will undoubtedly again leave you abruptly, but before *Mochet's* incubus comes to her on its nefarious errand. Keep vigil with me below her window, if you can bear it, *mon camarade!*"

As the subtle *Duc* had proposed, *Marie* and *Hatch* left the *château* late in the morning in the splendid, pristine, open-topped, vintage roadster. It was a glorious day. They were bound for *Minerve*, that ancient *Cathar Cité* and renowned beauty spot in the nearby mountains.

The others held counsel.

"I have learned the blasphemous contents of Skerne's scrolls," began the *Duc* in his deep, resonant baritone that had never sounded so grave. "In them is a ritual, which allegedly is the means whereby the Incarnation of the Godhead in the Womb of a Virgin can Occur. A ritual, I call it…more a bacchanal…an orgy…for at its culmination, the chosen maiden, driven insensate by wine, drugs, chanting, and dance, pleasures herself with Skerne's obscene Talisman! Its very depravity reeks of the sulphur of Hell! But by implication, it utterly desecrates the most sacred, Christian beliefs!"

The *Duc* paused as his shocked audience assimilated what he had just said.

"There is more. The scrolls allege that this ritual has only ever been performed once and that…abysmal heresy…Our Saviour Jesus Christ was the result! Yet worse follows! Should another maiden be found called Mary, the child of an Anna and a Joachim…" at this point all eyes turned towards *Anne* whose hand flew to her mouth to stifle a cry…"and if this Mary follows the ritual to its foul conclusion, if she too pleasures herself with Skerne's abominable artefact, then this will bring about 'The Second Coming!'"

The Author wishes to interrupt his narrative at this point to ask his Dear Reader a question. Has the Dear Reader ever considered the choice of the 8th of December as the Feast of The Immaculate Conception to be a tad (etc.) incongruous, given that the Feast of The Nativity is on the 25th? It gives Mary a gestation period of only seventeen days, close to that of a hamster.

Unless, that is, there is an assumption[51] that she gave birth in the December of the following year. But then *that* gives her a gestation period of three hundred and eighty-two days, which is longer than that of a Blue Whale and very close to that of a donkey!

However, there is a Satanic school of thought, which maliciously claims the Immaculate Conception actually took place on the morning of April Fool's Day—pernicious mischief, no doubt, though, alas, biologically much more tenable...

Of this profanity the *Duc* is cognizant.[52] He will make passing reference to it shortly, as we return to our narrative...

"The scrolls say, however," the *Duc* went on, "that this ritual can only be repeated in a year...here I quote... 'the sum of the digits of which having been reduced to a perfect number.'

"I must admit that puzzled me for some time, but I think I have the answer. Take this year, 1976. The sum of its digits is: $1 + 9 + 7 + 6 = 23$; $2 + 3$ reduces to 5. However, take next year, 1977. The sum of its digits is: $1 + 9 + 7 + 7 = 24$; $2 + 4$ reduces to 6, and 6 is a perfect number, both the sum and the product of its other factors each give us $6 - 1 + 2 + 3 = 6$; $1 \times 2 \times 3 = 6$...and forget at your peril that three sixes are the 'Sign of the Beast'!

---

51   No pun intended...really!
52   The Duc's encyclopaedic hoard of arcane knowledge is renowned.

Both *Hatch* and *Alexandrov Slivovitch* had a frisson of horror at this reminder.

"I believe, however," continued the *Duc* to an audience now totally in thrall to his knowledge, "that this is some consolation. This ritual cannot take place for at least five months. But I have good reason to believe…I will not explain why now…that in fact it will not take place until the first of April next year.

"There can be no doubt that Our Sovereign Lord and Creator has never been and would never be collaborative in any way with this…this…abomination. *Sacre Bleu!* He would have no need.

"But let us consider one thing: *Mochet* worships another and altogether different Lord…no, indeed, two things: *Mochet* is an Adept with awesome powers who could subvert and corrupt this ritual to his own ends…*non, je m'excuse,* three things: his Infernal Master would not fail to seize such a golden[53] opportunity. *Anne, Mochet* has not simply drugged, abducted, and hypnotised your daughter to spy on us. He has done so in order to summon her back into his clutches when the time is ripe. *Marie* would not simply be debased by this foul ritual, her body could become utterly defiled by the child she could then be carrying!"

The Second Coming! All were horrified by the slant the *Duc* had now given to that apocalyptic event! But none more so than the *Duc* himself! Comets, eclipses, signs, portents, the graves tenantless, the sheeted dead squeaking and gibbering in the streets, the rough beast slouching towards Bethlehem, silence in Heaven for

---

53   That *was* intended!

about half an hour[54]...Incredibly, suddenly, the erudite *Duc* himself was at a linguistic loss!

"What is the French for 'fretful porpentine'?" he wondered, as each particular hair upon his noble head stood on end, as he contemplated the sheer horror they could face!

"I have a plan..."

---

54   It's always a tranquil place, but we must assume a whole half an hour without a note from a harp or a whimper of ecstasy at the Beatific Vision is unusual!

Chapter Twenty-six

He said.

They had lunch, seated on cane chairs around a cane table beneath a vine-covered pergola in a shady corner of the magnificent grounds close to the *château's* imposing west wing. It was a welcome break.

No sooner was lunch over, however, than the good *Duc* resumed where he had left off.

"It is the bare bones of a plan, I fear. It has yet to be fleshed out with detail...and for that I crave your assistance." He paused for a moment. "When I took the commission to find Skerne's chest, His Eminence told me that Skerne's writings have not been studied since their acquisition by the local Bishop at the time of Skerne's death. Once the nature of their substance was known, The Holy Father at the time forbade any further research, and this interdict remains in force even to this day. So our knowledge must never go beyond this circle! But having learned that the contents of Skerne's chest are wholly evil, *I* have decided to destroy them...to put *Marie* or any future victim wholly beyond peril. But as the interdict *also* means that the contents of the chest will receive only a perfunctory check, I propose that we replace them with harmless replicas…so none other than us will ever know…"

He looked at the others quizzically. He need not have had the least qualm. Unanimously, they judged his plan a spiffing wheeze![55]

"How to do this quickly, however, is my immediate dilemma," he continued, "and the reason I turn to you all now for help! His Eminence is already apprised of the chest's recovery and awaits its delivery within the next few days. Speed is of the essence! For we cannot anticipate, either, how soon or even how *Mochet* will come baying at our heels!"

"In zat case, *Mon Cher Théodore*, I zink ve need to see ze contents of zis chest vizout furzer ado," said the astute *Alexandrov Slivovitch.*

Within minutes, the *Duc* had returned to their afternoon arbour with the damnable casket and carefully placed the malefic Talisman and the two, still-unfurled, accursed scrolls before his companions.

"*Oh là là!*" thought *Anne* when she saw the sizable golden todger, but deemed it prudent not to give voice to her reaction.

What occurred within the space of little more than a minute, though, filled the benign aristocrat with amazed gratitude.

"Ve can easily cast zat in plaster of Paris, and then spray-paint the copy to make it seem real," said *Alexandrov Slivovitch.*

"I've some primer and gold spray-paint in the garage," announced *Jean Le Taureau*, "from when I

55   Each, of course, mentally used his or her cultural equivalent of this apt and sterling phrase!

restored *Le Père Bénitier's* church candle holders last year. They looked like new. Everyone said so!"

"Ze weight vill be a problem. I need a piece of cast plaster of Paris—a mere cubic centimetre vill suffice—and I will vork out its specific gravity. Ve vill measure ze weight and volume of ze Talisman—ve vill employ Archimedes' principle, no? Zen I can calculate ze dimensions of a cylinder of heavy metal to insert wizin ze cast to replicate ze weight. Osmium vould be best. Can you source some for me, *Mon Cher Théodore?*"

"Get me some vellum, too, and italic pens, and I can write something that looks just like that," said *Anne*, pointing to the script. "I practised for hours when I was a girl!"

"We'll need to match those marks, as well," said *Jean Le Taureau* indicating the scratches and blemishes on the surface of the gold. "I'll photograph the thing from both sides. *Jean-Paul Lebouc* will develop them for me as soon as…! *Jean-Paul* and I were legionnaires together. He can be trusted! He just lives in the next village. Photography's his hobby."

"I can make the vellum look authentically old, too," *Anne* rejoined. "It's something I do with my younger students, have them make imitations of ancient scrolls. Its simple: a bit of cutting, tearing, folding; then a brief soaking in camomile tea and a blast from a hairdryer…"

"But what will you write?" asked an overwhelmed *Duc*.

Anne's eyes suddenly twinkled with mischief. "*Théo*," she said, "*Mathilde* showed me one of her cookery books this morning. You must make me a Latin translation of some recipes! I know! *Coq au vin, cassoulet, bouillabaisse,* and *tapenade! Voilà!*"

It was as though the delighted *Duc* had fallen for this bewitching woman all over again!

He clapped his hands. "Let's make a list of things to do, things to get, and the division of labour!" And so they did.

However, just as they completed it, *Alexandrov Slivovitch* asked the crucial question: "But, *Mon Cher Théodore,* how are ve to destroy ze Talisman itself?"

"I want it melted down, cast into ingots and each ingot sent to a separate, far-flung corner of the Earth!" replied the nettled nobleman at once. "Gold is a soft metal—we can easily saw it into pieces with a stout hacksaw! The melting point of gold is 1063° centigrade; even a pottery kiln gets hotter than that!"

No sooner had he said this than he rose and excused himself. "I must make a crucial 'phone call," he informed his friends and left.

Faute de mieux, the others poured themselves another glass of wine—savouring again the rich hints of nasturtium, nettlewart, and rhubarb—and awaited the resolute *Duc's* return. The *Cabernet monocépage* was local; and the *Duc's* appraisal—that it was sensual...without being wanton—was, of course, faultless!

෴

When the *Duc* returned, *Jean Le Taureau* went in search of his camera. The photos were duly taken, and at once, he and *Alexandrov Slivovitch* left to deliver the negatives to *Jean-Paul Lebouc*. Thence to *Narbonne*, to buy quick-setting plaster of Paris, sundry modelling tools, italic pens, black ink and A4 sheets of vellum. With luck, the developed prints could be collected as they returned.

Anne went at once in search of *Mathilde* and her cookery books and to ask her to make a bowl of *tisane* and to let it go cold. The *Duc* went in search of a writing pad, pencils, rubber, ruler, and his Latin grammar and dictionary. The enamoured couple were reunited shortly beneath the pergola, and the *Duc* began his task, while *Anne* looked on admiringly.

The learned *Duc* was quickly into his stride, even taking minor liberties with the wording, changing phrases like, "When the garlic is…" and "Once the anchovies are…" and "When the flames have died down…" to, "The garlic having been pressed …" and "The anchovies having been diced …" and "The chicken having been *flambé*…"[56] to make it stylistically more like the original, even though in all likelihood nobody other than he would ever appreciate this…but such was the man's highly developed aesthetic sense and appreciation of *l'art pour l'art!*

The others returned two hours later. The photos had been developed and were wholly fit for purpose. The negatives had been destroyed. *Jean Le Taureau* had been characteristically persuasive; thus, *Jean-Paul Lebouc* was solemnly sworn to silence.

---

56   Ablative absolutes, every one!

In the meantime, the well-connected *Duc's* crucial 'phone call had been answered. The Osmium had been sourced in *Perpignan*. The forge where it was now located merely awaited the specifications; thereupon, the Osmium could be milled by tomorrow, mid-morning!

Because of his missing digits, *Alexandrov Slivovitch* had to instruct *Jean Le Taureau* through the steps that needed to be taken. But the faithful factotum's manual skills were as the power of the Bentley he drove…First, using an empty matchbox, *Jean* constructed an open-topped receptacle one cubic centimetre in volume. Next, he filled this with a plaster mix which, when it quickly set, allowed *Alexandrov Slivovitch* to determine the material's specific gravity. A fish pan, a measuring jug, and some kitchen scales borrowed from *Mathilde* were all else that was needed to measure the Talisman's volume and weight. The scientific ex-soviet then quickly deduced how much the plaster facsimile would weigh!

At once, the brilliant ex-Bolshevik's brow knitted in concentration as he mentally did a series of more complex calculations. Finally, he announced, "Mes amis, zis is to some extent an estimate, but zat does not matter! Ze weight vill *feel* right. Gold is heavy but Osmium is heavier, vhich is as needs be, for it must take up less space!" Whereupon he told the *Duc* the diameter and length of the cylinder to be turned from what indeed was—as *Alexandrov Slivovitch* had of course known from the outset—the heaviest of all metals! The decisive *Duc* wasted not a second in forwarding this information to the forge! The bonus he had promised made him confident his orders would be ready on time! Orders, plural, for it would cast the ingots too!

The work continued apace, though the *Duc* had a growing anxiety that they might be surprised by the return of *Hatch* and *Marie*, when they were in a state of unpreparedness, and their ruse would be rumbled! Miraculously, a call from *Hatch* told them that he and *Marie* intended to dine in a restaurant in *Béziers*.

And so the work continued to continue apace!

At *Alexandrov Slivovitch's* request, the *château* was scoured for a vessel of the appropriate dimensions. It was *Mathilde*, who was again the provider—a biscuit tin from her *cache* of empty containers and receptacles! And after a further request, a bottle of washing-up liquid and some greaseproof paper too!

Still following *Alexandrov Slivovitch's* ingenious instructions, *Jean Le Taureau* coated the biscuit tin with washing-up liquid, and then poured into it a layer of plaster mix sufficient to cover half the circumference of the golden phallus, now also coated with washing-up liquid. Similarly coated greaseproof paper, which had been carefully cut, was laid around the exposed profile of the Talisman and across the whole surface of the plaster. Then more plaster was carefully poured to completely cover the Talisman—they had cast a mould.

An hour later, when the plaster had set, they were able to separate the two halves easily; the washing-up liquid had prevented adhesion.

The insides of the mould were now soaped before being filled with plaster. Next, a cardboard spool from a toilet roll was cut and rolled more tightly to just slightly more than the dimensions of the Osmium cylinder. It, too, was soaped, and then painstakingly twisted into the still-soft plaster inside the mould. The inside of the spool was carefully scooped empty with a spoon. The whole was left to set. An hour later the mould was carefully removed to reveal a perfect plaster imitation of the original. The tube of cardboard was gently prized from the interior of the cast, leaving a cavity that would receive the milled Osmium.

Spontaneously, the others rapturously applauded the resourceful Russian!

Anne realised that *Alexandrov Slivovitch,* together with his more than able assistant, had set the standard to which she must now aspire. She took all her materials up to her bedroom, which also had an antechamber containing a superb, mahogany *Louis XV escritoire,* not unlike the *Duc's.* Here, she could work without distraction and probably, as dearest *Théo* had before her, well into the night! *Mais quand même!*

The hour she spent there before dinner was preparatory. First, she had successfully tinted and dried the vellum. Then she had faintly ruled pencil lines onto each sheet to replicate the width, length and number of lines on the originals. She had planned the arrangement of words again to match the originals; and then with the aid of scissors and a modeller's scalpel, she had reproduced exactly the folds, nicks and tears in

Skerne's own scrolls. Finally, she was ready and relieved to be summoned to dinner.

"Maybe Joachim had a point!" she thought when *Jean Le Taureau* proposed to her a restorative *pastis*. A double would relax her and unfetter her creative flow!

Mathilde now served her contribution to the communal effort. Baked oysters and fennel; venison fillet, cooked *à point* in a pepper and mustard sauce, served with caramelised chicory and *pommes de terre dauphinoises*. Cheese followed—*mais bien sûr*, this is France; they have a type for every day of the year! But finally came a *millefeuille* in chocolate sauce, each of *Mathilde's* own preparation! *Délicieux!*

The *Duc* had served a subtle *viognier blanc* with the oysters; then, again, his splendid vintage *vin rouge* with the main course and cheese; a delightful *muscat* with the dessert; and his velvety *armagnac* with the coffee.

So what if *Alexandrov* and *Jean* had set *Anne* a challenge! Thus fortified, never had she felt more prepared to meet one!

Chapter Twenty-seven

Marie and *Hatch* returned serendipitously just as the *armagnac* had been placed on the delicate, taupe, linen table cloth, draping the highly polished, olive wood table at which the others were seated in the *château's* majestic *salle de banquet.*

Her day savouring the exhilaration of the *Bugatti*, the beauty of the region, and the warmth of the *Languedocian* sun, and *Hatch's* love had given *Marie's* skin a bloom and her eyes a lustre that, together with her informal attire, made her seem a Venus in blue jeans! "Oh *Maman*," she gushed, "today was perfect! We've been to places *you* would love, too! Not just for how nice they are, but all that history, as well!" And she joyfully catalogued her day in detail.

It grieved the *Duc* and *Anne* in equal measure to see her so happy and, at the same time, the object of their deception. But with that pertinacious perspicacity that so characterised the man, the *Duc* was able to keep wholly in focus the loftier, benign purpose of their actions; and also knew, as he had reassured *Anne*, that he had the means to free *Marie* from *Mochet's* evil influence and that he would do so very soon!

So, his hypocrisy was tempered by genuine benefaction when he proposed that *Marie* and *Hatch* should again take the *Bugatti* and explore *Carcassonne* and its *Cité* the next day.

"*Maman,* how was *your* day?"

"Lovely, *Ma Chérie,*" responded *Anne.* "I spent time with *Mathilde* in the kitchen, time with *Théo* in the garden, enjoyed two delicious meals"—here *Anne* patted her exquisitely flat stomach and abdomen—"enjoyed my book while *Théo* took the Talisman to the local church vault for safekeeping...he intends to take it back to England very soon, maybe the day after tomorrow..." *Anne,* too, had been able to misinform her daughter with nary a blush by also focussing on the greater good she thus hoped to achieve!

Now, with no further dissimulation needed, an hour of happy conversation could ensue, until, borne quite distinctly through the still and balmy night, came the chimes of midnight from the distant church clock. Abruptly, *Marie's* demeanour wholly changed. Her face assumed a mask-like immobility, her eyes became distant and vague, and she rose and left for her bedroom with the most peremptory "goodnight." Even though anticipated, nonetheless it still left the others unsettled and *Anne* and *Hatch* quite distraught. The *Duc* had to be at his most eloquent to reassure them both.

Then, recalling the task that faced her, *Anne* also took her leave. She and the *Duc* had a few brief moments alone together, during which again they kissed but went...no further! *Anne* entered her bedroom and began her hours of painstaking work.

Thereafter, *Alexandrov Slivovitch* and *Jean Le Taureau* also took to their beds.

At once, the shrewd *Duc* quickly told his loyal American friend all the events of the day. The two men then stole stealthily to the same place of concealment the *Duc* and *Anne* had occupied the previous night.

Nor had they long to wait! *Marie* opened the shutters of her bedroom, and swathed in her alluring night attire, stared into the foliage of the nearby tree.

Eventually, the *Duc* and *Hatch* could discern on one of its branches yet another of *Mochet's* infernal *incubi*, its tiny eyes glinting with unimaginable malevolence. This time, the Noxious Necromancer had summoned for his fell purpose a polecat—that most lonesome of creatures!

Almost immediately, *Marie* began to speak. "I cannot see anyone...I don't think I am overheard." A pause. "I have spent the whole of the day with the American." Another pause. "We have held hands. Yes, we have kissed...but, no, certainly not...no further! I would not allow it! I keep myself for the greater destiny for which you have told me I am intended. I realise this is imperative!" A third pause. "You want to enlist *him* in your service too? You wish to meet him? Tomorrow, we are going to *Carcassonne* to look round the *Cité*...Oh, I see, you will find us there yourself! Very well." A long pause. "The *Duc* has taken the Talisman to the local church...It is locked in the vault there for safekeeping...He intends to take it back to England the day after tomorrow..."

Marie fell silent. At once, the two men saw the foul thing in the tree scurry to the ground and vanish into the night. So, it had heard all that it had come to hear! It had also heard what the *Duc* and *Anne* had intended it should!

The sombre duo returned to the interior of the *château*. The *Duc* saw at once that the huge American's fists were clenched, his jaw set tight, and his eyes ablaze with anger.

"Come," said the *Duc* softly. "It is time now to take steps to free *Marie* from this ignominy!"

Together, they went up the *château's* magnificent sweeping staircase to knock on the door of *Marie's* bedroom. The sound jolted *Marie* from her trance and left her wondering why she was standing before the opened windows and shutters of her room, before she then began to wonder who might be knocking, wondering if indeed it might be *Hatch*! Nor could she understand the strange conflict in her mind. One part of her wanted to say to him, "One night with you would make my dreams come true." Another part of her felt compelled to say, "I hear you knocking, but you can't come in!" The sound of the *Duc's* deep, reassuring, baritone, however, telling her that both he and *Hatch* would like to talk to her seemed in some inexplicable way to break a spell!

Marie appeared before the two men, still delectably dressed in her diaphanous *robe de nuit*, through which was gloriously discernable a tasteful, *cérise* ensemble of negligée, bra, and culottes, which only partially covered her voluptuous shoulders, arms, breasts, buttocks, thighs, and calves. Within a trice, both the *Duc* and

Hatch had noticed these things. However, they dragged their thoughts[57] back to their more noble purpose.

Now, more decorously and less distractingly wrapped in a white, towelling dressing-gown of the *Duc's*, seated at the magnificent olive wood table in the *château's* majestic *salle de banquet, Marie* was learning all!

"What must I do?" she asked, finally.

"Submit to be hypnotised by *me*," replied the *Duc*. "I may first of all learn more of *Mochet's* intentions, but then liberate you from this monster!"

Marie slowly nodded and then reflected. "*Théodore*," she asked eventually, "would it be useful to leave me half in touch with *Mochet*, as it were...to still speak to him at night and go on feeding him what we want him to think...but being beyond his power to summon me away, as you fear he can? Is this possible? Could you do that?"

The *Duc* and *Hatch* simultaneously were seized with a proud and humble appreciation of this entrancing young woman. But for the overwhelmed American, even though for him *Marie* already had, she seemed to become all over again so very much more than just his latest flame!

It was agreed. The patrician polymath gave *Marie* a natural and harmless sedative before he began his fateful essay. Once assured she was totally relaxed, he lifted from around his neck the cross and chain made of the noblest of all metals, which he always wore, and began. Never had his deep, resonant and wholly seductive baritone been put to better use; never more appropriate

---

57   Which for moments were floridly prurient!

his choice of instrument. *Mochet's* machinations would be dismantled by means of the most sacred of symbols! The *Duc's* voice was a soporific susurration; the crucfix's oscillations, a mesmeric motion. Within a minute, *Marie* was in deep hypnosis.

What the *Duc* learned confirmed much that he had suspected! It seems *Mochet* had accosted *Marie* in *Le Cul De Blaireau*. She had been too polite to refuse his offer of coffee. She remembered that it had had a strange taste...then he had begun to swing his pocket watch. Next, she recalled she was in his car...then in his house...there was an exotic young man there too...she had been told to speak to his emissaries after midnight each night, but to remember nothing of this during the day. If his and her paths crossed, she would not recognise him...but if he said, "Do you enjoy a game of patience?" she would immediately take the pack of cards he had given her from her handbag and begin to play. When she turned over a Queen of Hearts— there were thirteen in this particular pack—she would obey any instruction he then gave her. It was imperative she remained *virga intacta*. She was destined for an exalted purpose! She was to become the mother of a very special child! *Mochet* had needed, too, to borrow her scarf...then she had been driven to the end of her mother's street, and *Mochet* had finally instructed her to remember nothing of what had occurred whilst in his presence!

The *Duc* then painstakingly obliterated or overrode every unseemly command and suggestion *Mochet* had implanted in this young woman's psyche—save one. The very one *Marie* herself had intrepidly suggested they should for the time being keep for their own better purpose.

He also ordained that she *should* remember everything that had transpired during this session… except for two things. First, he archly commanded that, when he proposed she come with them to England, she would accept without demur. If this happened before the *Duc* had had time to explain things to her mother, *Marie* would use this rationale: currently England swings like a pendulum do; this is the best of times to go there; it is too good an opportunity to miss! The *Duc* would explain all to *Anne* as soon as he could.

Second, when he pointed out that she would need her passport, *she* would propose to *Hatch* that they leave their visit to *Carcassonne* for another time and go instead to her apartment in *Montpelier* to get it…for the *Duc* was sure from what he had heard during *Marie's* earlier entrapment that *Mochet* was already in the area and intended to intercept *Marie* and *Hatch* in *Carcassonne*. So the further away from that place they were the better! *Mochet's* powers were still not to be underestimated! Also, now, until the contest with *Mochet* was wholly at an end, the good *Duc* wanted to ensure that she had their utmost protection! For that, she needed to be constantly in their presence!

The *Duc* released *Marie* from her trance. He gently probed her with questions. Her answers assured him his intervention had been wholly successful.

Marie had worn her hair differently that day, knowing she would be in the Bugatti, and had had no chance yet to unloosen it. Now, she smiled the sweetest of smiles. Because of this happy conjunction, she seemed to the *Duc* to be a Mona Lisa in a ponytail! It was great reward when she laid her hand gently on his arm and murmured, "Thank you so much, *Théo*. It feels already as though a great cloud has passed away."

"*Je t'en prie!*" the delighted aristocrat replied; and then after the briefest of pauses, he said, "Now, please excuse me. I would appreciate a longer sleep tonight. *Bonne nuit.*"

The *Duc* saw *Marie* turn to *Hatch* and hold out her hands for his, and a noble joy welled in his breast for them both. As he left the magnificent *salle de banquet* and began to ascend the splendid, winding staircase to his room, he reflected that he had wholly liberated this young woman this evening. So, earlier that day she and *Hatch* had held hands...they had even kissed...now perhaps tonight they might...go further...

A meaner mortal in the *Duc's* present position might have felt a nagging twinge of envy at the thought...but not the magnanimous *Théodore de Cornsai-Tantobé!*

Chapter Twenty-eight

Unusually, the *Duc* and *Alexandrov Slivovitch*, both, found themselves agonisingly on the horns of a dilemma during the course of the following morning, though for very different reasons...

On waking, *Alexandrov Slivovitch* had inexplicably recalled something in a recent scientific journal, which he had read in the reception area of the clinic while he was waiting for the results of *Marie's* toxicological screening three days ago. The article was about recent discoveries in human biochemistry. The recollection had led to a "Eureka moment." The last piece in the jigsaw of the complex, undetectable toxin he was devising suddenly fell into place.

However, maybe half an hour after he had triumphantly finalised its chemical formula, the exiled Russian read some appalling news in the morning paper.

On August 28th the odious leaders of his former homeland intended to test a nuclear bomb in *Kazakhstan*! Why? They knew their horrendous devices worked! The rest of the world knew their horrendous devices worked and, moreover, knew *they* knew their horrendous devices worked! So what was the point? More Strontium-90 in our bones? More leukaemias in our blood?

For the second time in three days, a monster from his subconscious unexpectedly possessed him, obliterating all else from his thought except blind fury! *Alexandrov Slivovitch* at once made a 'phone call to Russia.

"The *Yeltsin* Household," said a female voice.

"Is *Boris* there?"

"Who is this?"

"It is I, *Alexandrov Slivovitch Romanov!*"

"I am not sure that *Boris* would wish to speak to you…do you know that he is now First Secretary of the CPSU of *Sverdlovsk Oblast?*[58] He should have no dealings with defectors…"

"Is he there?"

A pause, then, "Yes."

"Then at least ask him…please!"

There was a longer pause, before *Alexandrov Slivovitch* began passionately outlining to his old drinking companion his plan to lace all of the *Politburo's* brimming, privileged glasses of premium vodka with his wholly undetectable poison. It might avert this damnable detonation! It would be long-overdue recompense for their indifference to his and his shipmates' fate! Hopefully, it might even sweep away the regime forever!

The response *Alexandrov Slivovitch* received made him grind enamel from his teeth. The nuclear test and its ramifications were not a major concern. Change was afoot, but now it was possible for the right leader to achieve it from within. He, *Boris*, was on his way, and he could indeed one day become that leader…and also he most strongly objected to ruining good vodka! The

58   Mm!

answer was no! Nor did he want to hear from *Alexandrov Slivovitch* ever again!

"*Boris*," mused *Alexandrov Slivovitch* wryly, as he replaced the 'phone, "always such a ludicrous name! God help Russia should it unbelievably ever elect that man as President! God help *anywhere* that elects anyone with such a name…"

Already, the incandescent ire from his Id was subsiding and the rational man he nearly always was re-emerged. *Alexandrov Slivovitch* felt a resigned relief that, at the eleventh hour, he had stepped back from the brink of the moral abyss that had engulfed *Brutus*…he would go to confession very soon and gain forgiveness for even having thought such a thing. He would confess, too, what he had done to that poor, misguided youth two days ago. Concern about his own wholly atypical behaviour fuelled his growing sense of remorse about that deed! And even if events kept him from the confessional, just having had the intention to go would be seen in the all-forgiving Creator's eyes as contrition! This was hugely reassuring!

Meanwhile, the devout *Duc* found himself teetering on the brink of an altogether different, moral abyss. He was a catholic; *Anne* was a *divorcée*! This chasm yawned ever more precipitously the more connubial bliss seemed to beckon! As always, from the time he was very young, whenever he was troubled, "*Théo*" sought the solace and sage advice of *Mathilde*.

"You soft lump," she said, immediately after he had unburdened his soul. "Do you think the good God sees things the same way that wrinkled, celibate, old prune in Rome thinks He does? Of course He doesn't! He knows the goodness of your heart! Can you not remember even when you were just a lad you gave up your pocket money for lepers and black babies in Africa?

(It was true. While still no more than a youth, the iconoclastic *Théodore* had begun to consider that it was possibly unacceptable to stereotype all blacks as cowardly, dim-witted, and lazy! In fact, he had around the same time begun to admire their native sense of rhythm and innate athleticism—as well as, of course, their naturally sunny dispositions! So he had begun his charitable acts towards them. But also, he had decided that when he became *Duc*, if a black family ever moved into the vicinity, he would set an example to the rest of the local population—as indeed befitted his station, how ever *passé* certain people nowadays might deem that aristocratic ideal to be—and so not only would he make a point of speaking to them if they passed in the street, he would even have *Mathilde* prepare a *pot-au-feu* from the Christmas dinner left overs and have it sent to them as a token of his warm acceptance of them into the community!)

"*Théodore*," continued *Mathilde*, "*Anne* is wholly delightful, and so is her daughter, who, moreover, could make *Hatch* your son-in-law! Have you considered that! I fully approve of them both! Besides, you deserve some happiness after all the sadness you have borne. You have been so stoic. Also—if you still have scruples—

don't forget that you have made the Nine First Fridays![59] The Lord has promised that you will have the chance of absolution before you die...and if push came to shove, *Didier* would absolve you any day of the week, anyway, of that I've no doubt. *Mais sacre bleu*! If I was The Almighty, I'd give you a lifelong Plenary Indulgence[60] just for the work you are carrying out on behalf of His Church at this very moment!"

The *Duc* was assuaged; the cloud had lifted! Marvellous *Mathilde*! And so the *Duc* unrestrainedly embraced *Anne* when she came down, somewhat belatedly, from her bedroom.

At the breakfast table, she displayed the results of her nocturnal handiwork to the impressed gathering. The counterfeit scrolls would, without a shred of doubt, pass muster.

Earlier that morning, *Jean Le Taureau* had sawn the Talisman into six roughly equal pieces and then hammered the malleable metal out of all resemblance to its original shape. Within perhaps an hour, he would return with the milled Osmium, having delivered the gold, and their plans would be all but complete.

"*Marie*," said the *Duc* at this point to his other delightful guest, who seemed more than usually radiant this morning, and before whom they all could now be completely open, "in a day's time, we leave for England. For your safety, I think you should come with us."

---

59   If you attend Mass and Communion on the first Friday of nine consecutive months, then God will guarantee your sins will be confessed and absolved just before you die. Not a bad deal really!
60   A full pardon of your sins—you skip Purgatory completely and go straight to Heaven. Worth having!

"*Oh, merveilleux! Merci!* I've always wanted to go there! *Mais alors*, England swings like a pendulum do…"

"*Mais alors, Ma Chérie, pas de conneries!*"[61] interjected *Anne* in her flawless French. "You'll be going to Yorkshire!"

The *Duc* averted a potential *contretemps* by quickly adding, "*Marie*, you will need your passport."

"Of course," *Marie* responded immediately. "*Hatch*, it's in *Montpelier*…we can always go to *Carcassonne* another time…"

"Sure," replied the somewhat spent American on cue.

◆

An hour later, *Hatch* and *Marie* were speeding ever farther from *Carcassonne* and *Mochet* in the vintage roadster. *Jean* had returned with the Osmium. *Anne* had carefully rolled her counterfeit scrolls and bound them with the original thongs. The Osmium had been inserted into the false Talisman and packed with newly mixed plaster, and the weight felt—like Baby Bear's porridge—just right! All that remained was for the new plaster to set, a little final sanding, then the coats of primer and finish, and the simulation of a few minor imperfections. All should be completed by noon!

On a sudden, generous impulse, the noble *Duc* suggested to *Mathilde* that she took the rest of the morning and afternoon off. He would take the others out to lunch beside the *Canal Du Midi*. He knew a

---

61   Roughly: "Ey up, Pet, no bullshit …"

little restaurant there that served superb seafood, whereupon *Anne* asked *Mathilde* for use of the kitchen later. *She* would like to prepare them all—*Mathilde* and *Didier* included—a special evening meal! She and the *Duc* would get what was needed later that afternoon. Then she realised that she, too, had spoken totally on impulse! Oh dear, had she possibly overstepped the mark? She looked anxiously at the *Duc*; and that's all it took...yes...just one look...And indeed, the *Duc's* heart had leapt with unbounded joy when she had made her proposals!

The gratified *Mathilde* set off to lunch with her priestly cousin, *Didier Bénitier*.

The others set off to savour the Mediterranean delights served in the *Duc's* chosen venue. The sky above them was a radiant blue; the warmth of the August sun enwrapped them like a cosseting quilt; the plane trees lining the embankment of the canal were a striking patchwork of creams, yellows, coppers, and tans; and all around them the grapes burgeoned in velvety, purple clusters. *Alexandrov Slivovitch* also knew that the levels of Strontium-90 in the vines themselves had fallen significantly, and the incidence of all types of leukaemia across the whole of the *Languedoc* was at its lowest for over a decade. So, for each and every one of them, just then, Life felt Good!

For the evening meal, *Anne* had decided to prepare an *hors d'oeuvre* of braised fennel in an *anisette* sauce,

and to serve, as the main course, pheasant breasts
cooked in a white wine, cream, and orange-pulp sauce
accompanied by *mange touts* and sautéed potatoes. She
would make *crème caramel* for dessert. She hoped all went
well. She wanted *Mathilde* to both approve and enjoy it.
While *Alexandrov Slivovitch* read in his room and *Jean Le
Taureau* enjoyed a *siesta*, the *Duc* took *Anne* on their first
shopping trip together in his majestic *Citroën DS*.

Having unpacked their purchases in the kitchen,
Anne was about to begin her preparations and the *Duc*
to go to his cellar to select something *very* special for the
evening, when the 'phone rang.

The Duc answered it.

"*Monsieur Le Duc de Cornsai-Tantobé?*" asked a man's
voice. It was a voice the good *Duc* did not recognise, but
already he was uneasy. The voice had a rasping, sibilant
quality, like the croaking of a toad, and it had made
even the simple enquiry redolent with menace.

"*Oui,*" replied the Duc.

"*Enchanté!* I am *Gaspard Mochet*, and I will come
straight to the point. You have taken from me something
that I want returned—now I have taken something from
you that I suspect you will want returned. Oh, you have
been cunning, *Monsieur Le Duc*, I'm quite impressed,
feeding me misinformation through the medium of my
little *Marie*. She and the American did not visit the *Cité*
in *Carcassonne* today, did they? You had not put Skerne's
chest in the church vault, had you? *Non!* But your little

act of *noblesse oblige* this morning has betrayed you. You have delivered to me instead *Mathilde*! Now *I* have a game to play!

"Please listen carefully to my instructions. First, go to the presbytery and untie that idiot priest—he will have exhausted all ninety plus elements by now! He will give you my written instructions, where you are to deliver the chest and its contents, where you will then be able to recover *Mathilde*. Do not suspect for even a moment that this is a bluff. The life of your housekeeper counts for nothing in *my* scheme of things, so do not make any attempt to try and outwit me further, or you will rue the day!"[62]

Mochet's call was at an end.

---

62   Another of the Author's own mother's most dreaded admonitions: "You'll rue the day, Our Tommy!" (Gulp).

Chapter Twenty-nine

It was a tight-lipped, ashen-faced aristocrat that returned to *Anne, Alexandrov Slivovitch,* and *Jean Le Taureau,* once the 'phone call was ended. The *Duc* related its gist.

"I fear I have been…how do the English put it? 'Too clever by half.' *Mais non*! Not clever enough by half! If any ill befalls *Mathilde*, how shall I ever forgive myself? This is my fault! I should have foreseen this and taken steps to prevent it! What should I do?"

There was a poignant moment of silence, poignant as only such a silent moment could be. It was *Jean Le Taureau* who finally spoke. "*Seigneur*," he said, "it is simple. What's in the chest is worthless. Just give it to *Mochet* and rescue *Mathilde*. Let's start work on another replica straightaway."

"But of course," interposed *Anne*, "we still have the mould, plaster, vellum, your Latin translations, camomile, washing-up liquid…"

"Ve will need more Osmium, *Mon Cher Théodore*. Can you arrange zis? Also ve vill need anozer chest."

Already, his *camarades* had lifted the *Duc* from his despair, and he had again become…proactive![63] It had

---

63   This word—original meaning "taking the initiative"—has enjoyed a vogue for some time among Educationalists. I'm not certain all its users know its original meaning, but from the way they use it, whatever they think it means is clearly a very good thing to be.

occurred to him that there might be a suitable chest close at hand. "Excuse me," he said.

The vigorous *Duc* bounded up the *château's* magnificent, winding staircase to his bedroom and rummaged in the deepest recesses of his capacious, mahogany *Louis XV* wardrobe. He found there something untouched for some time. He emptied its treasured contents in a heap on the delicate, taupe linen sheets, draping his ancestral bed. Then he bounded vigorously back down the stairs, carrying under each arm both *his* chest and Skerne's.

The company of complicit compeers made a careful comparison of the two caskets. There were differences, but there were many more similarities. *Alexandrov Slivovitch* pointed out that the Cardinal had probably only ever had a glimpse of the chest, anyway, and that its guardians had probably never closely inspected it, either. He reminded them all of the interdict forbidding any perusal of its contents.

The main problem was that the *Duc's* chest just looked too new. It was *Jean Le Taureau* who proposed a solution. He had a friend—another ex-legionnaire—who now had a business building pine kitchen furniture. He only lived two villages away. Though all his tables, chairs, and dressers were built to the same specification, he stained some of them with "Antique Pine" varnish and then "distressed" them by flogging them with a bicycle chain. These "antiques" retailed for twice the price of their unstained, unmarked twins. He also made verdigris by soaking copper nails in vinegar, and then painted it on the locks and hinges. *Jean* proposed he could go and get

Tom Carr

what was needed from his friend at once—which it was
agreed he should.

The urgent *Duc* then immediately went to the
'phone. The number he needed—that of *La Forge Du
Mont Destin, Perpignan*—was at hand on the telephone
table. Within less than a minute it was arranged! Another
cylinder of milled Osmium would be ready for them the
next day, mid-morning, together with the gold ingots.
The bonus the *Duc* proposed for this expeditiousness
was gratefully accepted.

The *Duc* then set off hotfoot to the presbytery to
rescue *Didier*.

The now-undaunted *Théodore de Cornsai-Tantobé*
found the good priest strapped to one of the chairs in
the presbytery's dining–room. As he was being released,
Didier bellowed the names of several transition metals
with great gusto. Finally, though, the wholly focussed
nobleman was able to get from him the letter of
instructions *Mochet* had left for the rescue of *Mathilde*.

The *Duc* perused the contents of the letter. It contained
a map, directions, a location where to leave the chest,
and where he would find further directions to *Mathilde*.
The letter also contained an assurance there would be no
trickery, an insistence that the *Duc* do this alone, and a
time when this should occur. The *Duc* looked at his watch.
He had an hour! He set off hotfoot back to the *château*.

As it happened, at that very same moment, *Mochet*
was wishing he had scheduled the exchange of

booty and hostage earlier. He was having a decidedly uncomfortable time with his captive. It had begun almost immediately after her capture.

"*Monsieur*, where are your manners? We are in no way well enough acquainted for you to address me by my first name or use "*tu*"! I have called you '*Monsieur*'. Address me as '*Madame*', using '*vous*', if you would, please! Is that understood?"

For *Mochet*, it was as if his own mother had reappeared incarnate before him, with the feeling of debilitating inadequacy that entailed!

He had then conceived a counter-attack, to drug and hypnotise *Mathilde* as he had *Marie*. Thus, he would regain the ascendancy and also possibly prise from her more information about the machinations of the devious *Duc*.

"*Monsieur*, I beg your pardon, but, *vraiment*, this coffee is disgusting, I'm afraid I cannot possibly drink it. How did you make it? Show me. I can give you some pointers as to where you are going wrong."

Having failed in his attempt to administer her the Benzodiazepine, he decided to attempt hypnotism, anyway, without it. He took out his pocket watch and said, "*Madame*, look into my eyes," as he began to swing the anachronistic timepiece.

"Look into your eyes! Why on earth should I want to do that? It's years since I've wanted to look into a man's eyes; but I've noticed yours are distinctly unhealthy! Quite yellow! What you ought to do is take regular infusions made from seeds of the milk thistle—it grows everywhere round here. It's excellent for liver complaints! And cut down on *pastis*!"

And at that point, she had taken the watch from his hand. "Mm! Well, fancy that! My grandfather had one that was exactly the same as this…"

The determined *Duc* meanwhile would brook no opposition…he would go alone. "*Anne*," he said, with more confidence than in fact he felt, "get on with the meal. *Mathilde* and *Didier* will be here to enjoy it, I assure you." And so he left.

After *Mochet* had taken *Mathilde* to another location and 'phoned the *Duc*, the grief had begun again.

"*Monsieur*, I really do wonder about you! Never mind what you're up to at the moment, whatever that's all about—a mouldering old box full of a load of nonsense and a rude piece of sculpture! Really! But then abducting that lovely young girl, as well! You didn't really think you would be in there with a chance, did you? She can have the pick of the bunch, and no offence, *Monsieur*, but, really, you're not it…you must know that, surely… And worshipping Satan! Dear, dear, what on earth do you want to be doing that for?"

For a moment, *Mochet* had believed he could still regain the initiative. "Power! The only thing worth having!" he exclaimed as if it were self-evident. "I shall do my master a great service by bringing him into this world in human form. He will reward me bounteously!"

"Well, that's as it may be!" responded *Mathilde* dismissively. "Oh, dear! Men and their dreams of power! You poor, sad dears! Do you mind if I ask you some personal questions, *Monsieur*..."

For the second time that day, the *Duc* settled behind the single-spoked steering wheel of his sleek *Citroën* and waited for the car to rise. He had calculated the travel time to his journey's end in the nearby hills. He should arrive on time. After forty minutes driving, he reached the tiny hamlet named on *Mochet's* map and stopped to consult the instructions again. A kilometre or so beyond the hamlet there was a signposted intersection. His memory of what to look out for thus refreshed, he set off again and shortly reached the crossroads. He turned as instructed. He was within three kilometres of his destination!

"*Madame*," *Mochet* meanwhile was saying, "*vous êtes certaine*...that in men who crave power there is often this pattern of an absent or ineffectual father and a domineering, possessive or overprotective mother? Tell me again the examples you gave me? Hitler, Napoleon...who else?"

"*Mais si, je en suis certaine*! I mentioned Alexander the Great and the Emperor Diacletian, as well. From what you have just told me about your upbringing, if you ask me, you're a classic case!"

For moments, *Mochet* buried his head in his hands. "This is disturbing, *Madame*," he murmured, "I'm having trouble dealing with this..."

"*Monsieur*, forgive me," said *Mathilde*, "but it's very close to the time to collect the chest."

"Oh yes, the chest," said *Mochet* distractedly, and after picking up a pair of binoculars, shuffled slowly to the front door. He trudged almost disconsolately to his car and drove a couple of kilometres along the road to his planned place of concealment.

He had not been there a minute when he saw a sleek, black *Citroën DS* glide to a halt on the road some distance below his vantage point. A tall, elegantly dressed man presently got out of the car and went to its boot.

Mochet followed his movements carefully through his binoculars. The man—most assuredly his adversary, the *Duc*—opened the car's boot, and then paused to look around him. At once, *Mochet* lowered his binoculars. He did not wish the *Duc* to see a glint from their lenses.

The *Duc* took stock of his surroundings: a remote, flat field from which old vines had been uprooted but new ones not yet planted. At its farthermost edge, the ground rose sharply and was covered in a dense, evergreen scrub. No doubt *Mochet* was hidden somewhere there at that very moment, watching the *Duc's* every move. The malevolent Mephistophelian had picked the location well.

Mochet watched the *Duc* tread a tentative path to the middle of the field.

There, the *Duc* found the envelope containing further instructions. The *Duc* put the chest on the ground and immediately turned back towards his car.

When *Mochet* confirmed—by means of his binoculars—that the *Duc's* car was wending its circuitous way towards *Mathilde,* he began to make a careful descent through the scrub to the field. Soon he would put long kilometres between himself and this pestiferous foe.

Mochet scuttled down the field and reached the chest. He turned the key, swung back the lid and peered inside. There were the scrolls and the Talisman. He lifted the weighty object and gazed at it. As he did so, a fanatical light rekindled in his eyes and the whole of the left side of his face spasmed with antic tics. "Power! Mastery! Domination!" he croaked fiendishly. "Nothing can stop me now!"

Mathilde's influence was unfortunately fading and that of his infernal master sadly re-ascendant!

Wholly duped by the masterly handiwork of the creative quartet, *Mochet* returned the fake Talisman to its container, closed and locked the chest, and set off with his "prize" back to his car. He had far to travel. It would be little short of midnight by the time he reached home.

The *Duc* eventually realised that he had probably been within a bare two kilometres of *Mathilde* when he had stood in the centre of that field. But it was a good ten kilometres of road to get there. *Mochet* had cleverly planned how to be well clear of the vicinity when finally the *Duc* reached her place of imprisonment.

It was a remote, little farmhouse beside the road. The front door was ajar. The *Duc* entered cautiously. And there was *Mathilde,* serving—as it transpired—a calming, restorative infusion of St. John's Wort to an elderly, visibly shaken couple. The *Duc* learned they had been forced at gunpoint shortly after lunch into their own barn, and left there bound and gagged, until *Mathilde* had released them about fifteen minutes ago.

Once assured the couple had taken no lasting harm from their ordeal, *Mathilde* and the *Duc* got into the *DS* and set off back to the *château*, to what would undoubtedly be a triumphal and magnificent meal.

"And are *you* all right, *Nounou?*"

"Don't be a soft lump, *Théodore!* Of course I am. You didn't think I'd let an odious little toad like that get under my skin, did you?"

And indeed—as a great affection filled his noble breast—the overjoyed *Duc* also felt a little abashed that he had ever thought otherwise.

Chapter Thirty

During his trip to and from his furniture-making friend, *Jean Le Taureau* had noticed on the plush, black carpet of the Bentley the reappearance of mysterious white flecks. Consequently, when finally *Jean's* rage was spent, the *Duc's* casket looked as though it had been the recipient of collateral damage throughout much of the hundred years' war. So, after coats of "Antique Pine" varnish and verdigris had been applied, it looked authentically old. And then paradoxically, after a sextuple *pastis*, the return of the *Duc* and *Mathilde* had brought tears of joy to the ex-legionnaire's eyes. *Mathilde* had seen this and was touched, and had surmised that, lurking beneath that intimidating exterior there was a smidgeon (etc.) of "soft lump." But wasn't it thus with all men?

So good was the meal—and indeed the whole *soirée*—that not the name of a single element escaped *Didier's* lips. *Mathilde* was appreciative; *Anne* delighted. But when the meal was over, for some there was still serious business to be done. Without a shadow of doubt, *Mochet* would ply *Marie* again for information. It was crucial he learned once more what they wanted him to know. So it was necessary for the *Duc* again to hypnotise *Marie*.

At half-past midnight, as the concealed *Anne Laverge,* *Hatch Beauchamp,* and *Théodore de Cornsai-Tantobé* had anticipated, another of *Mochet's incubi* came to communicate with the delightfully clad *Marie* from the tree opposite her window. Tonight, the evil emissary was a weasel—that most insinuating of animals!

Mochet's questioning began. *Marie* made her responses. "The *Duc* has sent his housekeeper and the priest to a flat he owns in Paris." Pause. "I do not know the address." Pause. "*Maman* may go there, too, or stay with me. We are leaving for England tomorrow." Pause. "Still? Of course! The *Duc* has to return the chest." Pause. "I don't know the answer to that question...all I can say is the *Duc* did chuckle during the meal tonight and say he hoped your Latin was good and that you liked *cassoulet, coq au vin, bouillabaisse,* and *tapenade*..." Pause. "I think we are going up the *Rhône* valley to *Calais,* as I understand..."

At this, the weasel melded with the night.

"*Mochet* will want to follow us," said the *Duc,* " so we will head west round *Toulouse* and up towards *Caen.* We will, unfortunately, still have to use *Marie* to keep him misinformed...but not for long." The *Duc* drew breath. "*Anne,* you could come too. What do you want to do?"

"*Théo,* taking me along would delay you. My passport is in *Nevers.* Besides, *Mathilde* has asked me if I would like to stay here until you return, to keep her company, help her in the garden...what do you think? May I?"

"Of course," answered the *Duc,* barely able to contain the soaring of his spirit.

The trio returned to the magnificent *salle de banquet*, and shortly, *Marie* joined them there. "How did I do?" she asked. "I assume it's happened...I came to, next to the window again..."

You were...*magnifique!*" said the appreciative aristocrat. "You told him everything we wanted him to hear. *Eh bien*, there is much to do tomorrow...*je vous laisse*."

"*Et moi, aussi*," said *Anne*. "I've got more forgeries to make. It'll take me quite a while..."

As they had the previous night, the *Duc* and *Anne* kissed, only to go again each to a chaste bed. *Hatch* and *Marie*, however, remained together, and a certain speculation inexorably resurfaced in the noble *Duc's* mind, resist it though he tried. As his two old friends already acknowledged, the *Duc's* fluency in English far surpassed their fluency in French, impressive though that was. So it is perhaps excusable—particularly given his long Yorkshire association—that his curiosity should be given crude, northern, Anglo-Saxon expression before even *he* had time to check himself.

"Is he giving her one? Is he getting his leg over? Is he getting his end away? Is he slipping her a length?" he wondered. "Does she shag like a rattlesnake? Does she bang like a shit-house door? Does she come like a factory hooter?"

Try as he might, this refined Frenchman who would never normally countenance such indiscretion, found himself unable to completely suppress such uncouth conjecture.

Nonetheless, he still remembered to scoop from the delicate, taupe linen sheets, draping his ancestral bed, the treasured contents of his now-distressed chest and to put them into his suitcase. He had already considered that a use might well be found for them very soon.

Meanwhile, *Mochet* was wringing *Marie's* scarf, while the left side of his face twitched uncontrollably. Recipes! Plaster of Paris! That afternoon he'd had the devious *Duc de Cornsai-Tantobé* within pistol-range! He should have shot him! So, they were heading for *Calais*, were they? Or was this more misinformation? On a hunch, *Mochet* decided that, first thing that morning, he would set off towards *Caen*. It was probably more practical for them to take the western route to the Channel! If they wanted to make haste, they would avoid *Millau*, of course...but, anyway, if he was mistaken, it would not matter too much...he knew their ultimate destination, and that of the chest. Hadn't he already wrested it with consummate ease from its keepers? And *Marie* was still his to summon when he wished!

The *Duc's* speculation was rekindled when, like the previous morning, *Marie* seemed more than usually radiant and *Hatch* unusually shagged out as they sat around the breakfast table! But perhaps, the good *Duc* told himself, the fresh air was helping *Marie* sleep well;

and maybe *Hatch* was overdoing his matinal exercise regime. Who knows?

Final preparations were completed. *Jean* had returned with more milled Osmium and the Gold ingots. The former was now inside the second fake Talisman; the latter in the *Duc's* secure and well-concealed safe. Soon, lepers, black babies, and other of the deserving needy in remote third world hovels would be the beneficiaries of Skerne's erstwhile golden willy.

Farewells were made. Flora McFlintloch had been told their probable time of arrival at Throstlenest Hall (and the *Duc* had learned that *Tristan* and *Iseult* were still well). The *Duc* had contacted the Cardinal and arranged a rendezvous in Darlington for delivery of the chest. Five rooms had been reserved for the night in "*L'Hôtel de la Reine*" in *Le Mans*. The Bentley was once again fleck-free. Benefiting from its more than adequate power, the five intrepid travellers were making good speed towards Northern France by eleven that morning. The car seated them all comfortably, even with the hulking *Hatch* in the rear next to his *Marie*!

They dined simply, yet well, at a roadside, rural *auberge*. They entered the suburbs of *Le Mans* just after six.

Jean Le Taureau's navigational skills had been flawless. After negotiating the town centre, he made a left turn and saw the hotel into which they were booked in the square before him; and he was pleased. He needed the toilet and he was relishing the prospect of a *Gauloise* and a *pastis* very soon.

Just as he was about to cover the final few metres of their journey, however, a crowd spilled onto the road. There at the forefront was a figure *Jean* particularly reviled. Perched on its head was a tall, black top hat. The *con*[64] sported a white vest with blue stripes, partially covered by a black, buttonless bolero jacket. It wore tight fitting, white flared trousers and footwear resembling ballet slippers. Its face was coated in white make-up, except where slashes of black covered its eyebrows, the sides of its eyes, and its lips. It seemed to be slowly stroking an imaginary, flat surface with both hands, as it deliberately blocked his way, to the crowd's great amusement. Clones of this insect infested most French towns and cities! *Jean* had decided that if ever he became *Président De La République*, not only would he be tough on mime, he'd be tough on the causes of mime! He'd exile *Marcel Marceau* to the nethermost reaches of the Sahara!

"*Du calme, mon vieux,*"[65] murmured the *Duc* in his persuasive baritone, and his stalwart steward responded; such was the circumspection *Jean* had acquired! But inwardly, he was still seized by a murderous rage. Calmly, he waited till a way opened through the throng. He drove the Bentley sedately into the hotel car park and dispensed his luggage-bearing duties. But no sooner were the cases stowed in their respective rooms, and his voluminous bladder voided, than he reconnoitred the immediate vicinity for an opportunity. He smoked a Gauloise and swigged liberally from his hip flask, as he did so, and as luck

---

64   Pillock.

65   Steady on, Old Boy.

would have it, he discovered something that gave his rage full, creative outlet: a partially constructed, four-storey commercial building with open access that nonetheless had display windows already installed on the ground and first floors. Surreptitious inspection inside this shell of a building revealed the presence of further means to wreak his vengeance! When he re-emerged into the street, he saw that the crowd around the *crétin* was starting to disperse. Very quickly, the square was empty, save for his target, which locked and picked up its collection box. *Jean's* good fortune continued. The grub set off in *Jean's* direction. *Jean* merged with mystic swiftness for one so big into the shadow of the building's door well.

He waited with the taut patience of a cat about to pounce. His prey was before him, and at once seized, dragged from the street, and manhandled up the concrete stairs to the first floor. *Jean* pinioned his catch against the window and quickly wound some rope tightly around each ankle, leaving generous lengths at each side. "Turn round or even move and you'll regret it," growled the seething ex-soldier to frightening effect. The end of each length of rope was then tied to a breezeblock, on top of which were piled several more. The *bestiole* was effectively tethered to a spot against the window. *Jean* took the top hat and left it in the street below the window, as a final, ironic gesture in this wholly appropriate act of moral equilibration. Hugging the side of the street to avoid identification by his victim, *Jean* stole back to the hotel and enjoyed another celebratory *Gauloise* and *pastis* before his evening meal. He had worn his chauffeur's gloves throughout. *Fait accompli!*

The Talisman of Skerne   by Tom Carr

He'd be tough on mime; he'd be tough on the causes of mime...

252

Jean wasn't to know that a second crowd gathered sometime later and applauded the superbly convincing portrayal of distress the mime artist was giving. In fact, his day's takings doubled, though this was small consolation. Three hours elapsed before two passing *gendarmes* went to arrest him for trespassing and exceeding the bounds of his licence. Unfortunately, he hadn't had a proper glimpse of his assailant and so couldn't give the *gendarmes* a description. He was traumatised, tearfully embarrassed by the discoloration of his trousers. Mercifully, he couldn't see the state of his mascara.

Jean found a growing dismay among the others when he returned from his own little mission. So enraged had he been on first entering the hotel that he had failed to notice what was now apparent. Its new owner was a rabid "Queen" fan, and "A Night At The Opera" was starting to play a second time over the establishment's sound system. When at half-nine "Bohemian Rhapsody" resumed for the fourth time, the *Duc* would have willingly paid a fortune to whoever would spare him his life from this monstrosity. Mercifully, the music stopped at ten.

Soon afterwards, the *Duc* again hypnotised *Marie* in preparation for *Mochet's* infernal interrogation.

And at half-twelve, the others watched, grim-faced, from the darkness at the other end of her bedroom as she went trance-like to the window, opened it, and faced the bat that hung in sinister vigil from the guttering of the adjacent wall.

Marie listened attentively for a few seconds before she spoke. "I knew nothing about the change of route, until we were in the car." Pause. "We are presently in a hotel in *Le Mans*." Pause. "Yes, I am in a single room." Pause. "The *Duc* says we will take the ferry from *Caen* to Portsmouth tomorrow." Pause. "I have no idea if he's telling me the truth." Pause. "He did say the crossing takes a few hours, though, and that we would have to stay in a hotel en route the following night." Pause. "No, I've no idea where."

Ensconced in a hotel room in *Rouen*, *Mochet* twisted *Marie's* scarf as he thought. He could be in *Caen* well before them tomorrow, but was that in fact where they would go? On a hunch, he decided he would go instead to *Le Havre*.

⚜

Once the *Duc* retired to his room, he too spent some time in thought. *Mochet* clearly distrusted the information *Marie* was now giving him. He would assume a change of route. What would *Mochet* guess was the most convenient alternative? Probably *Le Havre*. The *Duc* pondered a few moments longer and then decided that, in that case, they would still go to *Caen*!

⚜

Friends and foe alike were en route in good time the following morning. Soon into his journey, however, the Machiavellian *Mochet* had a further hunch. His antagonist was probably capable of even greater wiliness. With barely a second thought, he turned towards *Caen*.

At almost the same time, the super-subtle *Duc* had a similar thought. "*Jean*," he said abruptly, "head for *Le Havre*!"

Chapter Thirty-one

Yet how fickle are the tergiversations of Fate! The destination of each ferry from the two separate ports was the same! Both were sailing to Portsmouth! And even though *Mochet's* had the longer crossing, a curséd anomaly of timetabling made *his* the first to dock!

He sat patiently in his car at a convenient vantage point and, as he constantly twisted *Marie's* scarf between his annelid fingers, he watched the procession of disembarked vehicles emerging from the terminus. *Et voilà!* Ludicrously conspicuous amid the Ford Cortinas, Austin Allegros, Renault 4s, 2CVs, and VW Campers was an opulent Bentley! And though there could have been little doubt who would be in it, clearly visible beside the burly chauffeur was the Infuriating Aristocrat himself, while in the back, between the dark, disfigured Russian and the preposterously well-sculpted, dentally endowed American sat the lissom *Laverge* girl!

Mochet emitted a croaking chuckle of satisfaction. Surreptitiously, he merged into the flow of traffic, one car behind the limousine. He had both the Talisman and *Marie* back in his sights and close at hand! Excellent! He had so much more now than the glimmerings of a plan that should return both to his clutches that very night!

Alexandrov Slivovitch had been lulled into slumber by the motion of the car. The *Duc*, too, felt drowsy…though for some time he had been kept awake by occasional snatches of the fond whisperings that passed between *Marie* and *Hatch*.

"*Hatch*, it's just so counter-intuitive, how the electron can be in more than one place or follow different trajectories at the same time!" sighed *Marie*—talking now bewitchingly about the book she had just finished reading.

"I know," he breathed back to her with a passion that was almost palpable. "In my field, relativistic effects… like time dilation and the contraction of length at very high velocities…these can seem just as baffling…"

"Mm!" she murmured with melting sweetness.

It gladdened the good *Duc's* heart to hear this ultra-dimension to their love—the pearl of intellectual compatibility! A calm settled upon his soul, and for a while he, too, slept.

He was roused by the low, gruff voice of his chauffeur. "*Seigneur*, forgive me, but I think we are being followed."

It took the *Duc* a moment or two to gather his wits, assimilate what he had just heard, and respond. "*Comment?* Why do you think that?"

"*Seigneur*, if I may…I suggest you don't turn round now…but two cars behind us there's an orange *Citroën GS*. It has left-hand drive and a French number plate. It moved into position when we left the ferry terminus in Portsmouth, and it's stayed there ever since. If I slow down, it slows down; if I pick up speed, it picks up speed. I cannot get a clear view of the driver because of the glint from the windscreen and the extra car's distance he manages to keep between him and us, and besides, I've never seen this *Mochet*...but I'm sure that car is following us! And who else could it be?"

Moving his eyes but not his head, the *Duc* looked in the Bentley's left wing mirror and saw the car in question. As *Jean* had said, it was impossible to clearly see its driver...but as *Jean* had observed, too, who else *was* it likely to be?

"Indeed!" responded the *Duc*. "*Jean*, what would you propose?"

"Do you want me to lose him, *Seigneur*?"

The *Duc* reflected a moment. "Please. I think that would be best."

"Then leave this to me!"

Jean had executed the manoeuvre he had in mind more than once. All he needed was a suitable roundabout. And how glad he was to have every last smidgeon (etc.) of the Bentley's more than adequate power at his disposal. The *Citroën's* modest motor could not compete! Every fibre of *Jean's* being now tingled with anticipation.

They came to a roundabout within two minutes, but it had only three exits. The Bentley remained sedately *en route*. Five minutes later, *Jean* saw the sign for another roundabout, and this one proved ideal. It had five exits, a large circumference and a dense, mature shrubbery covering the mound at its centre. *Jean* indicated right and moved into the outer lane. He set off slowly round the roundabout, as the orange *Citroën*, too, indicated right and moved out to follow him. As the Bentley turned out of the *Citroën's* line of vision, *Jean* immediately unleashed his vehicle's prodigious power and swept right back round the roundabout, then slowed and sedately took the exit onto their original, intended route.

Mochet came round the island to find that the Bentley was nowhere in sight. Which exit had it taken? As he slowed, looked, and dithered, horns began to sound. He could have believed himself back in France. He was finally hemmed into going back the way he had come, and it was more than five minutes before he reached the previous roundabout and could again reverse direction! As soon as he was able, he pulled into a lay-by, consulted his map and again began to try to double-guess where his enemies would be heading now.

"Well done, *Mon Brave!*" said the delighted *Duc*, as the now-unfollowed Bentley sped on its way. "*Eh bien*, let's go in search of a place to spend the night. Let's show *Marie* a glimpse of the delights of Oxford!"

Meanwhile, *Mochet* seethed. If it hadn't been adulatory in his perverse lexicon, he would have called the *Duc* just then a very fiend from Hell! But summoning to his aid a real and most dread beast from the Abyss was what the thwarted Malignity judged would now better serve his increasingly urgent purpose and bitter lust for revenge! He had made a portentous decision!

And having persuaded himself that this latest setback would be merely temporary, *Mochet* resumed his journey north and eventually booked into a country inn close to Bicester. He learned that the locals rhyme Bicester with "blister"[66]—and how resonant, given the pustulous swelling on the rump of Humanity that would be lodged there that night!

It was *Marie's* first visit to England. Even though she knew a mere thirty-four kilometres of water separated the two countries at their closest point, everything around her seemed wholly alien: the layout of the roads, borders, hedges, and fields; the appearance of the quaint, thatched cottages in the villages through which they had passed; the sights, sounds, and smells of Oxford and of the interior of the pub where they dined; the flavours of the food and the beer, the very gestures and manner of the people. She was fascinated. She grilled the *Duc* avidly about everything she noticed and was totally enthralled by what he told her about the wildness of the Yorkshire Dales and the rugged splendour of Throstlenest Hall that she could expect the following day. Finally, she was utterly incredulous

---

66   Also to further fuel *Mochet's* bewilderment at English orthography, the proprietor, whose name on the sign over the front entrance, was spelt "Menzies St. John Featherstonehaugh," introduced himself to his guest as "Ming Singein' Fanshaw." It may possibly also be the quirky pronunciation of his middle name that has led the English to adopt St. John as the patron saint of burn victims.

when he told her she would also meet two three-toed sloths. It was as if the suave, urbane Gallic aristocrat she had so recently come to know and appreciate had suddenly transmuted into a whimsical, Anglo-Saxon eccentric just by breathing the very air of these isles! Would it affect *her* too this way? And the prospect of becoming different, even ever so slightly mad, excited her strangely. Maybe, indeed, this was how it started... though *her* choice would not be the sloth; it would be the aardvark...which never did anyone any harm.[67]

Late into the evening, however, more sombre considerations inevitably intruded. For what would now be the penultimate time—the *Duc* assured *Marie* that he was certain of this—*Théodore de Cornsai-Tantobé* hypnotised her.

The *Duc* primed *Marie* again with what he wanted *Mochet* to believe—most importantly that the Talisman was with him and would be so for several days more, until the Cardinal came to retrieve it. He primed her also to withhold things he would rather *Mochet* did not know... but this second category was more problematic. The *Duc* could not predict all the questions *Mochet* would ask!

And, indeed, the *incubus* that *Mochet* sent that night—a sinuous and sinister stoat—was intermediary to a long and searching interrogation...

---

67   Not, of course, that *Marie* supposed for a moment human history was littered with victims of the vicious depredations of sloths. *Non*. It was simply another case of "*chacun à son goût*."

After listening to it for anxious minutes, the *Duc* finally felt no really serious damage had been done, despite the additional and sometimes surprising information that *Mochet* had wanted from *Marie!*

The *Duc* could surely never have suspected, though, that his ownership of a slothery—upon which *Marie* had been asked to elaborate as much as she could— would appear to *Mochet* as an unexpected and fortuitous *Achilles' Heel,* and indeed confirm the aptness of his earlier, ominous decision!

Nevertheless, later, in the solitude of his hotel room, the good *Duc was* uneasy. *Mochet* was probably now becoming desperate and had awesome powers at his disposal. Even though the *Duc,* Adept that he was, felt he could thwart them and was, indeed, close to laying waste the whole of *Mochet's* nefarious scheme…yet, still, a tiny kernel of doubt nestled in his musings, and he half-recalled a further measure he might have at his disposal to put things right if all else failed. And then, at this eleventh hour, the erudite aristocrat's memory failed him…He knew the name of the rite he sought, but could no longer remember its content…He realised he would have to look further, and the need was now pressing!

At this point, it is wholly appropriate to digress a tad (etc.), as will become clear in due course.

By the end of the Second World War there were seventeen branches of Military Intelligence, numbered one to nineteen. It was largely supposed even by all the other branches that MI13 and MI19 had never been allocated any function. But with the utmost secrecy, MI13 *was* given a commission, and had as its head an old friend of the *Duc*—dear old "Melmers"—better known to the world at large as Sir Melmerby Wath, renowned cricketer, playwright, and scholar, whose life the *Duc* had once undoubtedly saved when he had exposed and foiled a diabolical plot masterminded by the dastardly Staple Fitzpaine,[68] landowner, industrialist, playboy, and Black Magician, who had long been on "Melmers'" radar!

The ultra-covert operation "Melmers" headed in MI13 was designated "Supernatural Hostile Activity Management" (SHAM); and no one was better qualified to lead it, "Melmers" being as adept an Adept as the Duc himself! Though now retired, Sir Melmerby Wath still had a vast network of contacts—both corporeal and non-corporeal—and therefore huge influence. It was to dear old "Melmers" that the *Duc* had made those crucial 'phone calls at intervals in our narrative. Sir Melmerby also had probably the most comprehensive, private library of esoteric literature in the whole of Western Europe, and it was due to this that, soon, *Théodore de Cornsai-Tantobé* would call on one last favour from his old friend! For where else could the awesome *Duc*

---

68   See "Black Rites In Barnstaple" by the same author.

refresh his inexplicably flagging memory and find this final means of reassurance?

Agitated, unable yet to sleep, the *Duc* decided a draught of night air would be beneficial. As he stepped into the corridor, he saw *Hatch* about to enter *Marie's* room. His huge friend saw him, stopped, and then stammered: *"Marie*, I've got to a really gripping chapter in *my* book…it's all about the differences between Freud and Jung…I just had to tell you…"

"Oh. *Hatch*, don't be so silly! The *Duc* understands… he is French!" Whereupon, she smiled and waved to the *Duc*, seized *Hatch's* hand, yanked him across her threshold, and closed the door.

The *Duc* smiled wryly, as he continued on his way. An apposite French aphorism popped into his head as he did so: "*Canard chanceux!*"[69]

The five intrepid friends left Oxford just after ten the following morning. In less than four hours time, *Alexandrov Slivovitch, Hatch,* and *Marie* should be installed in Throstlenest Hall. *Jean Le Taureau* would then take the *Duc* on a further journey to Darlington to deliver the chest. If all went well, the five of them would eat that evening in The Dingleberry Arms, and no doubt in his

---

69   "Lucky duck!"

irresistible French accent, *Jean* would propose things to Betty which she would not resist.

About the same time as the Bentley purred out of Oxford, the Abominable Blister left Bicester.

Friends and execrable foe alike were heading inexorably to a do-or-die *dénouement!*

Chapter Thirty-two

The game that, regrettably but necessarily, the *Duc* had had to play out with *Mochet* through the medium of *Marie* was close to its end.

Even before they had gone out to dine, he had hypnotised her a final time and unravelled the last vestiges of evil, wholly freeing her of *Mochet's* influence; he would be unable to summon her to his foul ends. The *Duc* had only to ensure that this night she would also be free from any other peril.

Marie was ready for bed, delectably draped—the *Duc* again noticed—in her diaphanous *robe de nuit*, through which was gloriously discernable a tasteful, *cérise* ensemble of negligée, bra, and culottes, which only partially covered her voluptuous shoulders, arms, breasts, buttocks, thighs, and calves.

He and his friends accompanied *Marie* to her bedroom[70]. When they entered it, *Marie* was as astonished as the American and the Russian to see that her bed had been moved to the centre of the room. There was the bewildering presence, too, of lots of small, oval pieces of silvery metal. *Marie* could have had no way of knowing, but these were nearly the whole of the *Duc's* treasury of Miraculous Medals, gifts rained on him over the years by black babies' families and grateful lepers.

[70]   The *Duc* had explained to his two amorous guests—with commendable delicacy, of course—why he had given them separate rooms.

Later, the *Duc* had had all these wondrous icons blessed personally by the Holy Father himself, and had stored them in the chest he had only recently surrendered to another, higher purpose! The sacred objects now lay in an unbroken, circular chain around her bed.

The *Duc* took a phial from his pocket and asked *Marie* to drink it. At first unsure—understandably so after recent experience—she eventually put her faith in this exceptional, wholly benign man, as she had correctly judged him to be, and drank the flask's contents. The *Duc* enjoined her to get into her bed. Again, she complied. Already, she was feeling drowsy. Within seconds she was asleep. He benignly beckoned *Hatch* to tuck her in and then the *Duc* gently crossed her forehead with a long, aristocratic index finger at the end of which were impeccably manicured nails. The three quietly withdrew. The *Duc* assured the others she would not awaken now for a good twelve hours.

But the *Duc* surreptitiously returned at a convenient moment later with a pitcher of Holy Water. The *Duc* slowly encompassed her bed, sprinkling the medals with the water, all the while intoning the words of an ancient, potent rite known by very few, even among the Adept! She was now wholly secure! This child of Mary—indeed a *Marie* herself—would benefit from the full weight of The Blessed Virgin's intercession with her Divine, Ascended Son! Assuredly, no harm at all would touch her!

How the *Duc* now hoped he could leave his two, dear friends as safe! For to some extent, that depended on them! He must trust them!

The *Duc* led them along the chandeliered corridors of the baronial edifice, for indeed, such it still was, into a room neither of his friends had ever seen before. It had once been a chapel, but the simple, wooden altar was long gone. The ceilings were exceptionally high and vaulted. The room was bare, save for five pewter urns placed around a circle drawn on the bare, stone floor, inside which was also drawn a pentacle, partially covered by two Dunlopillo airbeds with Force Ten sleeping bags upon them. The *Duc's* friends now noticed that the five pewter urns were positioned at each apex of the pentacle.

The *Duc* waved his hand at the five vessels. "Salt, pepper, olive oil, balsamic vinegar, and garlic," he said, in that deep resonant, baritone that was his alone— "traditional protection against ageless evil."

His friends suddenly saw the *Duc* more distraught than they had ever seen him before. There was a pause, pregnant in a way only such pauses can be.

"*Mes amis*," resumed the *Duc*, "*assurément* tonight *Mochet* will make his final play. *Alexandrov Slivovitch*, this is the endgame! It must be checkmate to *us!*"

For a moment, the noble *Duc* paused, seemingly even more distraught than instants before. "*Milles excuses*," he almost whispered, so restricted had become his throat, "but this could also be the most perilous night of your lives. Promise me, *promise me*, that the two of you will sleep on those Dunlopillo airbeds and *never, never* leave this circle till dawn! Should someone else appear to be in the room—*par example*, most likely *Marie*...do *not* believe it, and to confirm this, throw some liquid at the apparition from one of the jugs I will bring to you shortly—they contain a secret emolument, the constituents of which very few know, even among the Adept. But it has a potency beyond measure against all the Powers of Evil!

"*Marie* herself, I assure you, will be *utterly* safe; I have taken other, even more formidable precautions to make sure of *that!*

"*Jean* too will be safe; he has a job to do for me, which will take him away from here. Flora is safe in the cottage in Wangthwaite. *Eh bien, voilà.* But, remember, *please*, whatever you do, do *not* leave this circle!

"*Hélas, mes amis, I* must go to visit my old friend Sir Melmerby Wath who lives some distance from here, to consult some learned tomes that I can find nowhere else but in his library...This may take up the entire night... but cannot be delayed; otherwise, I would stay to see you through this most dire of dangers!"

The *Duc* left the room but returned shortly, bearing a tray on which were the four promised jugs. "Remember, follow my instructions to the letter, and you will be safe...*bon courage...au revoir...*" were his parting words.

Bewildered, but naturally trusting the *Duc*, the two stalwart companions lay down on the two Dunlopillo airbeds inside the strangely inscribed circle, and cosy in their Force Ten sleeping bags, they were, in fact, soon asleep.

How long they had slept, neither found time to check. A pervasive chill had awakened them both. At the same moment, they saw *Marie* before them. She was totally naked, her melon-like breasts full and firm, their wine-dark nipples luscious buds of desire, her figure voluptuous and lissom, her stomach exquisitely flat, her raven, pubic bush a veil that covered a dark tunnel of inexpressible delight. Thus, she appeared lubriciously before them!

"Come to me, *Hatch*," she panted, "my body craves you…"

In a sudden ferment of desire, still half-befuddled with sleep, *Hatch* rose randily from his airbed.

However, his Russian comrade was already more awake and—surprisingly—less tumescent, which was to their great, good fortune; for at once, he recalled the *Duc's* warning. He threw the contents of one of the *Duc's* jugs at this obscene simulacrum of *Marie*, which instantly faded from sight with a shivering wail…

"Lawdy Miss Clawdy, what the hell's goin' awn here?" drawled *Hatch*.

He was soon to learn more. Again, the room grew chill. *Mochet* in a last, desperate bid before the dawn was putting out all his power and had summoned to his aid a very fiend from Hell! Against the opposite wall, a swirling mist appeared, which gradually, terrifyingly took recognisable form. It seemed eventually to fill the whole room. It was *The Giant Ground Sloth of Popocatépetl*—one of the lesser-known but most grotesque incarnations of Satan himself! *Mochet* was seeking to exploit what he believed could be one of the *Duc's* few weaknesses, by sending an entity the *Duc* would be loath to harm! But he had miscalculated—the *Duc* was not there!

The Talisman of Skerne   by Tom Carr

The Giant Ground Sloth of Popocatépetl

Meanwhile, gripped with a totally unaccustomed terror, *Hatch* felt an overwhelming urge to fill his pants, but suddenly, mercifully, realised with timely prescience that, of course, this was another ploy on the part of their diabolical adversary intended to lure him outside of the pentacle, and he then felt a slightly smug, but wholly appropriate, gratitude for his daily exercise *régime* which had given him such tight control of his anal sphincter.

"My God," said the trembling *Alexandrov Slivovitch*, " I need a fag!" Despite being inside the *Duc's* house, he took a purple, golden-tipped *Sobranie* from its packet, placed it in his mouth, and lit a match (he always kept a packet of both in his pyjama pocket)...

Blinded by the light, *The Giant Ground Sloth of Popocatépetl* whimpered with pain. "Oh, stop it, stop it, that hurts! You bitch! Oh, I could scratch your eyes out! Stop it..." it hissed, gesturing impotently with its immense talons but unable to penetrate the protective sanctum of the inviolate pentacle.

"Strike a light!" shouted *Hatch*. *Alexandrov Slivovitch* needed no second bidding. He took a third and a fourth match from the box too, but the second was sufficient. With another shriek of pain and an evanescent "bitch" the huge, grotesque phantasm slowly faded from sight, even as the morning sun began to dapple the surrounding hills with its damask glow and cast its saving light into the room.

Dawn had come; they were safe. The brave duo had survived the ordeal. *Mochet* had failed.

Immediately, *Hatch* raced along the corridors of the *Duc's* antique edifice and burst into *Marie's* bedroom.

His heart surged with unbounded relief. She was unharmed, still blissfully...and beautifully...asleep!

In a state of befuddled joy, he staggered into the grounds of the *Duc's* Anglo-Saxon aestival retreat, and then, incongruously, with mounting urgency, raced to a tree behind which he vomited copiously.

His limping Russian ally saw most of this from afar (and guessed the rest) and a demon from his subconscious inexplicably rose to the forefront of his mind. Before he had time to check himself, the word "*ПуФФ*" had escaped from his lips. Immediately, he had regained composure and was hugely relieved no one had heard him!

Chapter Thirty-three

The *Duc* had returned to Throstlenest Hall, as soon as possible that morning and was overjoyed that all was well—even though of course he knew that it should be so if his instructions had been followed; and indeed why shouldn't they have been, given two such dependable allies?

The three friends—*Marie* was still asleep—were now seated in the breakfast room when the post arrived.

The *Duc* picked up with his well-manicured fingers from the pile of letters he had placed on the table beside him, the special delivery that bore the insignia of the Vatican! The trio looked at it with intrigue. The *Duc* opened the auspiciously marked missive with pleasurable anticipation[71] and read it. Unexpectedly, for his two friends, a crease furrowed his distinguished forehead. He let the sheet drop from his slender, aristocratic hand onto the delicate, taupe, linen tablecloth, covering the highly polished olive wood table, and a snort of derision exploded from his well-coiffeured nostrils that opened into his noble, aquiline nose.

"You might like to read this…Papal Bull!"

Never had the deep, resonant baritone issuing from the *Duc's* noble, perfectly proportioned mouth sounded more bleakly bitter to his two friends.

---

71 Possibly plenary indulgences for the three of them in recompense for their services?

But *Hatch* and *Alexandrov Slivovitch* knew at once the reason why, once they had digested the letter's contents! Either the *Duc* surrender the chest and its contents to the Holy See at once, or both he and his two friends would be assumed to be in breach of a Papal Interdict, the penalty for which was instant *excommunication*!

The *Duc* wasted no time in 'phoning His Eminence in Dublin!

But what he heard was chilling!

"The Holy Father believes *you* still have the chest, for nefarious reasons of your own. It was not difficult to persuade him, given your occult leanings! Who will he believe if you say not? You or me? You have been of good service to me, *Monsieur Le Duc*, but all your esoteric knowledge has not availed you in the end!"

(How gloating the envious, Celtic oaf had sounded when he had said that!)

"I have the Talisman and its secrets. His Holy Father is old and ailing. Perhaps when he dies, with Skerne's chest to aid my candidature, the College of Cardinals can be persuaded that next time would be a good time to elect an Irish Pope...I have long thought that the Blessed Virgin's family were probably Irish anyway... Mary...such a good Irish, Catholic name, don't you think? So I feel wholly justified! An Irish Pope, now! Oh, a very good thing, to be sure!"

The *Duc* slammed down the 'phone.

It took very little reflection for him to realise he had been both used and out-manoeuvred. While he'd been so focussed on *Mochet*, he'd failed to see the presence of another enemy! Bitter bile rose in his throat. He considered his options. The *Duc* could tell His Eminence that what was now in his possession was a fake...but so reveal his own duplicity, which would further fuel suspicion in the Vatican...but could the *Duc* risk anyway embarking on such a game of bluff and double-bluff and treble-bluff...who knew where it might end? Octuple-bluff? When at risk was not simply his friends' lives and his own, but *excommunication!* The consignment of his own immortal soul and *theirs* to everlasting damnation! Unless...it took only one beat of his heart for the *Duc* to opt for this once-only, desperate alternative...and how glad he was of last night's journey!

His two friends watched with astonishment when, suddenly, a furrow creased the *Duc's* regal brow. He closed his eyes in immense concentration, threw wide his arms attached to the end of which were hands with aristocratic palms, attached to the ends of which were long, elegant fingers with exquisitely manicured nails. All were now outstretched; and the *Duc* began to intone in that deep, resonant baritone that was his alone:

> *"Obla Di, Obla Da,*
> *Kumba Yi, Kumba Ya,*
> *Ze Di, Ze Dan*
> *Obi Wi, Obi Wan"*

The *Duc's* voice had grown unearthly and imperious, the room had become preternaturally dark and cold; and a sudden gust of icy wind swept over his two friends who abruptly lost consciousness.

The *Duc* looked at them both with a deep, yet wholly chaste, love and knew that his perilous gamble had been worth the taking. He had dared to recite in a language even more ancient than Latin—which now he could never do again—the last four lines of the *Satsuma Ritual*,[72] and so had altered the space-time continuum in miraculous and convenient ways!

The false Talisman was now secure in the original's undisclosed location but could never be a threat again to anyone! Stanley, the sexton of St. Polycarp, was sitting atop a *Kev*, and fluently outlining to Cheryl, the barmaid, sitting opposite him atop an *Alby*, the steps in his planned, new board game, "Orgasm."[73] ("Calvary" would be on sale shortly!)

The phobia-free Fr. O'Hegarty was installing beehives in his garden—the start of a new hobby—and looking forward to his first batch of mead fortified with *poteen*. The Cardinal's hubristic schemes were now as his island's blighted tubers during its infamous famine. The sect of Skerne was again a risible, insignificant bunch of *fous*. And *Mochet's* bloated, bufonide body lay flayed and lifeless in a godforsaken, fetid ditch. *The Giant Ground Sloth of Popocatépetl* had turned on the one who had summoned it from the Abyss and had exacted apt payment for such a fruitless mission...*Mochet's* immortal soul was even then beginning its eternal torment in the flames of Hell... this, the wholly appropriate, just conclusion to the *Duc's* daring, supernatural intervention to put things right!

---

72   The reader is strongly advised not to try this at home!
73   For example, landing on the square "Premature Ejaculation" sent you back to "Start."

Alexandrov Slivovitch regained consciousness and was instantly bemused to find that he was wearing an eye-patch, an unusually lined, single, sable glove and that next to his chair was an elegant, cedar wood cane. Why would he have need of any of these items, he thought, as he stood up, unaided, onto his two feet (one of which, though, was inexplicably shoeless and sockless)? He and everyone who knew him had acquired a selective amnesia—which would last the rest of their lives—about his previous injuries. He swept back his black, luxurious hair from his lean, refined, unblemished, attractive face with the five fingers of his now ungloved right hand and reflected that it seemed far too long since he'd enjoyed any female attention…indeed he felt wholly ready for a really good shag!

When *Hatch* regained consciousness (at virtually the same time) he remembered he had not exercised that morning. Excusing himself, he went back to his room, did his daily two hundred sit-ups, one hundred press-ups, and wonderfully, gripping solely with his teeth the strong, nylon cord he had slung over his door and tied to the banister beyond it, managed that tenth, elusive heave!

Also—unbeknown to the *Duc*—two missing teenagers from Darlington were reunited with their overjoyed parents, and the former rent-boy from *Marseilles* was reconciled with his father when *Julien Latapette* renounced his old ways and said he would begin training for the priesthood in Ireland.

An old woman with rickets in *Nevers* found her lost poodle.

A garden gnome salesman from Twickenham and a mime artist from *Le Mans* both recovered totally from their post-traumatic stress syndrome, though with the loss of any recollection of the cause. (It would be nice to say they then both resumed useful lives... *mais quand même*...)

An aging jogger in *Nevers* endlessly regaled whoever would listen to him how he had been revived from total cardiac arrest by the prompt action of a fortuitously passing paramedic!

Jean Le Taureau admitted finally to himself that he had an "anger-management problem" and was proactive in seeking counselling to address this.

Joachim Laverge's craving for *pastis* wonderfully disappeared, and his liver slowly but surely recovered. He became, consequently, a wholly happier horticulturalist...and much more likely to live to enjoy his grandchildren! However, all evidence (and memory on anyone's part) that he had ever actually *married Anne Laverge* vanished completely. So, if—or more likely—when the time came, the devout *Duc* (unlike many another aristocrat) would not have the thorny issue of a divorce with which to contend![74]

The *Duc* left his friends for a smidgeon[75] (etc.) of time and went to check on his two pets. As he entered the warm, humid slothery, he heard an unaccustomed, rhythmic wheezing. Alarmed, he looked urgently into

---

74   Notice the word order! One must never use a preposition to end a sentence with. And one must never start a sentence with "and" or "but." But also to tastelessly split infinites...well!

75   I am making an arbitrary decision: from smallest to largest, it's "iota," "tad," "smidgeon."

the foliage of the two secropias for its cause... *et voilà!* *Tristan* was slowly but determinedly rogering *Iseult* for all he was worth... *mais merveilleux!*

"Somethang ah got to ask ya, thow, yaw old raccoon," drawled the New Orlean's giant when the enraptured *Duc* had returned: "Wha's awl yer linen and drapes and so fawth tawpe? It's not something ah would truly a' bin bothered about mahself, yaw knaw, but *Marie's* bin intrigued...guess it's a woman's thang."

"How strange that you should ask that," murmured the *Duc*. " It's been very much on my mind of late. It was my late wife's choice. For years, I have not been able to bring myself to change it. I suppose I have preserved all this as a shrine to her memory. But I have decided the time has finally come to move on! Certainly, *she* would not have wished me to be in mourning for the rest of my life. Now, I suspect I'm going to give both Flora and *Mathilde* hours of delight discussing new decors with *Anne*."

At this, the American and the Russian exchanged approving looks, approving as only such looks can be.

"By the way," added the *Duc* to change tack, " you do know, don't you, that '*taupe*' is the French for 'mole'?"

"Nah, *Théo*, ah didn't know that!" *Hatch* exclaimed.

Alexandrov Slivovitch looked at the tablecloth then back at the *Duc*. "Really! But moles are not zis colour!"

"Nah! That's right!" said *Hatch*, then after a moment's reflection, he had another reflection: "Nah, ah awnly need look up the French fer manatee, okapi, wolverine, armadillo, slender loris, aind coypu!" he reflected.

"Some moleskins, you know," announced *Alexandrov Slivovitch*, "can be as fine as sable." He flexed his un-gloved, five-digit right hand then wondered why on earth he had told the *Duc* this; perhaps something still lurked deep in his subconscious? But by definition, how could he know?

"*Vraiment*, some moleskins as fine as sables?" intoned the *Duc* with genuine interest at learning this little-known fact, which wholly vindicated for *Alexandrov Slivovitch* his inexplicable (or should that be Freudian?) slip.

Suddenly carefree, the three of them soon began a breakfast of black pudding (*sang de porc coagulé*), chitterlings (*estomac de vache haché*), scrambled eggs (*oeufs brouillés en matière graisse*), haggis (*blague écossaise*) and royal porridge (*bouillie d'avoine au whisky*).

No sooner had they started, however, than *Marie* appeared before them already dressed in the jumper, cardigan, and woollen skirt her father had bought her. The temperature had plummeted during the night to a hyperborean 18° Celsius. She had even brought her scarf as an added precaution. The *Duc* noticed this last item with immense, inner satisfaction.

Then, with that customary *politesse* that was second nature, he excused himself briefly and phoned the prestigious *salon* where he had commissioned his little gift for *Les Femmes Laverge* of two sable overcoats and immediately ordered duplicates in top of the range moleskin.

Marie's dark, almond eyes were still glazed with sleep, giving them, for *Hatch*, a lustre more than usually intoxicating. She took a seat at the table and announced that she was starving. Her exquisitely flat stomach and abdomen were well nigh empty. She set about the *délices* with relish.

Tomorrow they would all set off in the still white-fleck-free Bentley for *La Belle France*. *Anne Laverge* awaited both her daughter and the *Duc* in *Le Château du Prat Ragé*—and, a week later, Betty would fly from Newcastle to *Perpignan* using a prestigious Irish airline to sample the delights of *Jean Le Taureau's pays natal...* *et en plus...*

Alexandrov Slivovitch decided he should get out more. He made himself a little, half-serious wager that, if *he*, too, hadn't got laid bloody soon, he would go back to Russia[76]...

Et enfin...

---

76 The reader will no doubt be delighted to know that *Alexandrov Slivovitch* is still enjoying all the benefits of Western Democracy! To discover how, where, when, and with whom read *Lucifer Wore Lycra* by the same author, involving our same three heroes: a rollicking roller coaster of a romp revealing cannibalism in Tunbridge Wells; theft of enriched uranium from Hartlepool; an outbreak of Bubonic Plague in Perpignan, in which the Vatican itself is implicated; and the emergence of *Shaka Zulu* with an *impi* through a portal in the space-time continuum to join the fight against International Terrorism in Africa...who better? And all set against the pulsating pace of the *Languedocian* leg of the *Tour De France*! An absolute must!

Glossary

Prologue

Cornsai-Tantobé—Cornsay and Tantobie are small, ex-mining communities in the northwest of County Durham.

Longueur—means both "length" and "tedium."

Sasha Distel—1933— 2004—originally an accomplished jazz pianist, jazz guitarist and writer of music, his good looks and seductive crooning brought him renown in the 60s, 70s and 80s, and he became one of a very few French singers to enjoy popularity outside of France. He once performed a private concert for the Queen Mother, and, also, allegedly had affairs with Brigitte Bardot, Francine Bréaud and Dionne Warwick.

Muckle—much, greatly (Scottish dialect).

Sae ferlie—so unusual (Scottish dialect).

Dinnae fash yersel'—don't bother yourself (Scottish dialect).

C'est déjà fait—it's already done.

Hautré-Wattisse—a wholly fictitious brand, created by "Frenchifying" the surnames of two British comic actors, Charles Hawtrey 1914—1988 and Richard Wattis 1912—1975.

Mullard's "Auld Arthur"—another fictitious brand based on the name of another British comic actor, Arthur Mullard 1910—1995.

Part One
Chapter One

Trimdon Colliery—Trimdon Working Men's Club was in the media's spotlights at each election that Tony Blair fought as Labour candidate for Sedgefield.

St. Polycarp—a second century Christian martyr.

Stanley Crook—a small village in Weardale, County Durham.

Waddingtons—makers of card and board games from 1922 until *Hasbro* bought them in 1994.

Vicar-General—a sort of Roman Catholic Bishop's "enforcer."

Bonilace—pronounced "bonny lass", Geordie dialect for "pretty girl".

Geordie — Geordie dialect for a native of Tyneside, and the dialect.

Chapter Two

Poteen—pronounced roughly "putcheen," a potato-based, (often illegally) distilled, Irish liquor.

Limousin—cattle originally bred in the *Limousin* area of France. Usually brown in colour, they are fine beef cattle now extensively interbred in England.

Tupping time—mating season.

Toxoplasmosis—characterised by swollen glands and flu-like symptoms, caught from contact with cat faeces.

Weil's Disease—characterised by high fever and headaches; it can lead to liver and kidney complications and even meningitis.

Chapter Four

N'importe—no matter
Limericks—as far as I know, the authors of the limericks quoted here are anonymous. The second, which doesn't rhyme, I first heard from my father over fifty years ago.

Chapter Five

Caruso—Enrico Caruso, 1873—1921, renowned Italian tenor.
The Wild Swans At Coole—a W.B. Yeats' poem.
Paisley—this is obviously a reference to the dog's wool-like fur, and in no way an attempt to associate the personality of the dog with that of the Rev. Ian Paisley, Ulster Unionist MP, and former First Minister of the Northern Ireland Assembly.
Cat Scratch Fever—a bacterial infection usually arising after a scratch from a cat.
Hieronymous Bosch—1415—1516, a Netherlands painter famous for his fantastic imagery.
Quebec—I do not know for sure which one is named after which, nor indeed if such is the case. (There is also a "Washington" and a "Toronto" in County Durham.)

Chapter Six

Boulvardier—man about town.
Pas du tout—not at all.
Ken Norton—he temporarily derailed Mohammed Ali's quest to regain the heavyweight championship of the

world by out-pointing him over twelve rounds in 1973. He broke Ali's jaw in the second round. Ali won a rematch after he had regained the title from George Foreman in 1974.

Chapter Nine

Ricardo Montalaban—a fine actor who played, amongst other things, Khan in Star Trek II "The Wrath Of Khan." *Gento* and *Puskàs* were both members of the *Real Madrid* team who beat *Eintracht* in the 1960 European Cup final, considered by many still to be one of the greatest exhibitions of team football coupled with individual skill ever seen.

Cépage—grape variety.

Heureusement—happily.

La rive gauche—the left bank (of *La Seine* in Paris—a trendy place to hang out, I'm told).

Couleur—colour.

Bouquet—"nose," aroma.

Hatch Beauchamp—a picturesque Somerset village just off the A358 near Taunton. Colonel Chard, hero of the Battle of Rorke's Drift—see the film "Zulu"—is buried there.

Bouchée—a mouthful.

Prénom—first name.

Mais comme d'habitude—but as usual.

Paysage—countryside.

Languedoc—the area of southern France between the Mediterranean and the Massif Central stretching roughly from the Cevennes and the Rhône in the east to the Spanish border in the south-west.

Château—castle. The majority of French *châteaux* do not in the least resemble English castles architecturally. French *châteaux* are turreted, country retreats rather than fortified strongholds. But are they worth seeing? Start in *La Loire*. Go and see *Chenenceaux*!

Prat Ragé—a "Frenchifying" of a quaint northeastern term: "radged prat" meaning, roughly, "a rather silly person." However, between *Narbonne* and *Perpignan* there is a place called "*Le Prat du Cest.*" I have no idea what, if anything, that means…or, alternatively, who he might be…

Un peu de trop—a bit too much; a bit "over the top."

Faites commes chez vous—make yourselves at home.

A demain—till tomorrow.

Impis—regiments.

Passe-temps—hobby.

Bagatelle—bagatelle, trifle.

Objets d'art—objets d'art.

Renier-Renato—a wholly fictitious brand (look up, however, the names of the duo who had a hit in 1982 with "Save Your Love" then say their names quickly in a French accent).

Chapter Ten

Sang de porc coagulé—congealed pig's blood.

Estomac de vache haché—chopped up cow's stomach.

Oeufs brouillés—scrambled eggs.

Matière graisse—fat (as in lard).

Blague écossaise—Scottish joke.

Bouillie d'avoine au whisky—boiled oats with whisky.

Une crime passionelle—a crime of passion.
Seigneur—Lord.
Bien sûr—of course.
Argot rimant—rhyming slang.
Fait accompli—job done.
Calvados—apple brandy from Normandy.
De toute façon—anyway.

Chapter Eleven

Hélas—alas.
Délicatesse—delicacy, refinement.
Moules frites—mussels and chips.
Apparemment—apparently.
Folie—madness.
Vraiment du progrès—real progress.
Bêtise—stupidity.
En plus—in addition.
Mais à plus tard—but later.
Digestif—a glass of strong liquor—brandy, whisky, calvados—taken after a meal.

Chapter Twelve

Des bonnes vacances—a good holiday.
Quinze août—the 15th August, the feast of the Assumption and a bank holiday in France; it is considered the unofficial end of summer.
Cuillère—spoon.
Le Cul De Blaireau—"The Badger's Arse"; any English reader who lives in a *cul de sac* may like to reflect that

he or she lives in a "bag's arse"—the French name is *impasse.*

Entrecôtes de cheval—horse rib steak.

Pastis—the generic name for all aniseed liquors like *Pernod* or *Ricard* (which are brand names).

Cuisson—how it is cooked

Ile flottante—literally, "floating isle"; poached meringue floating on custard.

Kir royal—cherry liqueur in champagne.

Pichet—jug, pitcher.

Exactement comme il faut—just right.

Ce n'est pas grande chose—it's no big deal

Incroyable—unbelievable.

Ça m'amuse tout simplement—it's simply a bit of fun.

Une agrégée—someone with a higher teaching degree. At the time that this story is set—1976—such a person would teach fewer hours than someone less qualified.

Amant—lover.

Chapter Thirteen

Non plus—(n)either.

Mais bien sûr—but of course.

Mon Dieu—My God.

De temps en temps—from time to time.

Un peu distrait—a bit distracted.

Mais aussi, chose incroyable—but an unbelievable thing, as well.

Mon affaire—my business.

C'est méchant—it's naughty.

Je vous laisse—à la prochaine—bonne continuation—I take my leave—till the next time—"have a good day."
Tarte aux pommes—apple tart.
Dors bien—sleep well.

Chapter Fourteen

Non, pas du tout—no, not at all.
Petit morseau de merde—little piece of shit.
Jouissance—orgasm.
Bestiole—insect, bug.
La Patrie—the Fatherland, i.e. France.
Une bonne dose—a good measure.
Fous—"nutters."
Alors, ça c'est autre chose—now that's another matter.
Inconnus—unknowns, strangers.

Chapter Fifteen

A son avis—in his opinion.
La douane—customs.
Complet—fully booked.
"...It was **now or never**! The *Duc* had to **surrender** to practicality, but he was adamant...**one night**! 'That's all right,' he told the others, 'but **no more**! That would be **too much**!'"—full marks to the reader who spotted that the *Duc's* little outburst contained the titles of six Elvis songs—the *Duc* had been affected by the ambiance of the hotel, clearly!
Eau de vie—literally "water of life"; a generic term for any strong liquor; "vodka" and "whisky" mean substantially the same thing in Russian and Gaelic.
Mais, regarde! Le nom!—But look! The name!

Chapter Sixteen

Pour manger—in order to eat.
A toute à l'heure—in a moment, shortly.
Politesse—politeness, good manners.
Chez elle—at her place.
Cuisses de grenouille—frogs' legs.
Crevettes à l'ail—prawns in garlic.
Шит—shit.

Chapter Seventeen

A bientôt—(see you) soon.
Après tout—after all.
Précieux—precious (young men).
Milieu—social circle.
Comment c'était formidable—"how great was that!"

Chapter Eighteen

Absolument pas—absolutely not.
Débloquer—to unblock; unjam.
Elle avait raison—she was right.
Allons-y—let's go.
Une douleur—sadness, pain.

Chapter Nineteen

C'est merveilleux—it's wonderful.
Jamais—never.
Mais vous voilà—but there you are.

Chapter Twenty

Milles excuses—a thousand pardons.
Je vous en prie—don't mention it.
Le mot juste—the right word.
Bufonide—toad-like (from the name of the family, *Bufonidae*).

Chapter Twenty-one

Mon, mon! Eh bien, j'irai au pied de nos escaliers—My, my! Ee well, I'll go to the foot of our stairs (a quaint Yorkshire expression of surprise).
Chacun à son goût—each to his own taste.
"*Quem spectas? Buccam pugni desideras? Dentes tuos custodire amare habebas?*" -"Who are you looking at? Do you want a mouthful of fist? Would you like to keep your teeth?"
Fonctionnaire—civil servant; state employee.

Chapter Twenty-two

Frottage—rubbing.
Tout simplement—quite simply.
Nounou—an affectionate term for "nanny."
Norman wisdom—on reading this, it is hoped readers will immediately make a humorous association. Otherwise the sentence was scarcely worth writing. Norman Wisdom —1915— 2010— was a popular English comedian, singer-songwriter and actor, best remembered for the series of films in which he played the hapless character, Norman Pitkin. However, he could be a fine, serious

actor too. He also had a successful run on Broadway. He received an OBE and later was knighted. [The best jokes are those you have to explain!]

Châtelaine—the female owner or mistress of a castle.

Chapter Twenty-three

Douceur—softness, sweetness.

Jack Johnson—1878 to 1946. For non-aficionados, *Johnson* was the first black heavyweight champion of the world and still considered one of the best. He was a defensive specialist in the ring and a controversial figure out of it. Even if you are not particularly interested in boxing, but *are* interested in social history, *Unforgivable Blackness* by Geoffrey C. Ward (Pimlico 2005) is well worth a read.

Mary Archer—wife of Jeffrey, Lord Archer, athlete, author, former Chairman of the Conservative Party, and Ex-convict. Mary testified on behalf of her husband in a libel trial in 1987 and so impressed the judge, Mr. Justice Caulfield, that he described her as "fragrant".

Dépardieu-Belmondo—*Gérard* and *Jean-Paul* respectively, renowned French actors.

Assemblage—blend.

Chambré—at room temperature.

Cigales—cicadas.

Cicadas—cigales.

Chapter Twenty-four

Mais maintenant! Alors!—But now! Well!

Chapter Twenty-five

Moue—pout, sulky expression.

Escritoire—writing desk.

Cerdan-Carpentier—another wholly fictitious brand, derived from the surnames of two French boxers; respectively, *Marcel* and *Georges*.

Marcel Cerdan—1916 to 1949—became middleweight champion of the world in 1948. He is also famous for his affair with *Edith Piaf.* Allegedly, he was the "love of her life." It was her one and only regret that he was killed in a plane crash the year after he had become champion.

Georges Carpentier—1894—1975—became light-heavyweight champion of the world in 1920. The following year he challenged *Jack Dempsey* for the world heavyweight title and was knocked out in the fourth round of what was boxing's first million-dollar gate promotion.

Moreno-Chakiris—*Rita* and *George* respectively, stars in the film "West Side Story"

Ne t'inquiète pas, mon brave—a closer rendition might be "Don't get yourself in a flap, old boy"…or maybe not.

From **"Comets, eclipses…"** to **"each particular hair"**—bits lifted from Shakespeare ("Hamlet"), Yeats ("The Second Coming") and St. John ("The Book of Revelation").

Chapter Twenty-six

Faute de mieux—for want of anything better.

Monocépage—wine made from a single grape variety.

Flambé—doused in brandy and set alight.

L'art pour l'art—Art for Art's sake.

Pommes de terre dauphinoises—the Author's favourite version is sliced potatoes, fennel and garlic cooked with cheese and cream.

Millefeuille—literally "thousand leaf"; a classic French cake served as a dessert.

Chapter Twenty-seven

"...**polecat** ...**lonesome**..." "Lonesome Polecat" is a song in "Seven Brides For Seven Brothers." More recently (1994) Gerry Rafferty did a fine, bluesy version on his album "Over My Head."

Je t'en prie—the familiar version of *"je vous en prie"*— "don't mention it."

Chapter Twenty-eight

Boris Yeltzin's promotion and the nuclear test both actually occurred in 1976. *Leonid Brezhnev* was Soviet leader at the time. *Mikhail Gorbachev* became leader nine years later.

Chapter Twenty-nine

Camarades—friends, comrades.

La Forge Du Mont Destin—The Forge of Mount Doom.

Mais si, j'en suis certaine—But yes (emphasised) I'm sure about it.

Chapter Thirty-one

Sir Melmerby Wath—Melmerby and Wath are two villages close to Ripon in North Yorkshire. Travellers on the northbound A1 might spot the sign to Melmerby and Wath twenty or so miles before Scotch Corner. It may also interest the reader to know that a family firm in Melmerby—"Bare Earth"—produces *biltong*, air-dried raw meat, eaten by Allan Quartermain, Sir Henry Curtis and Captain John Good RN on their expedition to "King Solomon's Mines"; and also a favourite of Liz Hurley, apparently, intrepid adventuress that she is!

Staple Fitzpaine—a Somerset village close to *Hatch Beauchamp* situated between the A358 and the M5.

Chapter Thirty-two

Assurément—for sure; certainly.

ПуФФ—Puff.

Chapter Thirty-three

Délices—delights.

Pays natal—country of birth.

Et en plus—and more besides.

Et enfin—and finally.

Shaka Zulu—1787—1828—military genius, dictator and founder of the Zulu nation. His adult life was characterised by a drive for power and domination, hardly surprising given the dominant mother/absent father pattern of his childhood!

Vocabulaire

Manatee	le lamantin
Okapi	l'okapi (m)
Wolverine	le glouton
Armadillo	le tatou
Slender loris	le loris mince
Coypu	le ragondin
Sparking plug	la bougie d'allumage
Head gasket	le joint de culasse
Timing belt	le pignon de distribution
Overhead camshaft	l'arbre à cames en dessus (m)
Piston ring	le segment de piston
Dipstick	la jauge d'huile
Grout	le coulis
Skirting board	la plinthe
Loft insulation	l'isolation thermique
Junction box	la boîte de dérivation
Guttering	les gouttières
Rawl plug	la cheville
Screwdriver	le tournevis
Spanner	la clef
Yak	le yak
Musk ox	le boeuf musqué
Potto	le potto
Platypus	l'ornithorynque (m)
Echidna	l'échidné (m)
Wombat	le wombat
Fly wheel	le volant de commande
Constant-velocity joint	le joint de cardan, joint homocinétique

Crankshaft	le vilebrequin
Tappet	le poussoir, le culbuteur
Anti-roll bar	la barre antiroulis
Damper	l'amortisseur
Wheel trim	l'enjoliveur
Wainscoting	le lambris
Beading	la baguette
Dowel	la cheville, le bois à goujons
Sander	la ponceuse[77]
Wood filler	le bouche-pores, le mastic
Drill	la perceuse
Drill bit	la mèche
Allen key	la clef
Plane	le rabot
Cement mixer	la bétonnière
Plasterer's float	la spatule
Pointing trowel	la truelle de jointoiement
Wallpaper scraper	le couteau de peintre
Wallpaper paste	la colle badigeon
Roller	le rouleau
Chisel	le ciseau, le burin
Extension lead	le câble de raccordement
Tile cutter	le tailleur de carrelage
Spirit level	le niveau à bulle d'air
Flamingo	le flamant
Fretful porpentine	le porc-épic grincheux

77　"To sand" in French is "poncer." Macho British builders in France have a bad time of it as a result. "*Ah, vous poncez! Poncez-vous souvent? Est-ce que vous voulez poncer chez moi ce weekend?*" This has become a standard chat-up line among French gays fancying a bit of Anglo-Saxon rough.

Useful, eh? Impressed? And just for good measure...

Three-toed sloth	le paresseux à trois orteils
Giant ground sloth	le paresseux géant terrestre

Bonne nuit. Ulala kamnandi.
(Goodnight. Sleep well)

Made in the USA
Charleston, SC
14 June 2011